PURSUING EXCELLENCE THROUGH OPTIMAL HEALTH AND WELLNESS

PURSUING EXCELLENCE THROUGH OPTIMAL HEALTH AND WELLNESS

Lloyd Bridges, MD

ISBN: 978-1-09832-620-3

Table of Contents

Introduction

AS A DIPLOMATE OF THE American Academy of Family Physicians
with over twenty-five years of ambulatory care experience, I grew
up in a family of health care providers. Pursuing excellence was
pursuing a career in medicine. In 1960 my dad was the first black
ob-gyn resident at Jackson Memorial Hospital in Miami, Florida,
and my mom was a registered nurse. My siblings and I were blessed
to grow up in a very loving family where academics were empha-
sized. Sandwiched between my older sister, Sabrina, and younger
brother, Mark, I made sure my parents knew I always sought to
shine in their eyes.

As a good-natured child growing up, I spent endless summer
days and nights over my grandmother's house with my cousins—
long, hot summers in Miami, playing pranks on one another;
playing football or kickball in the street; playing hide-and-seek
from dawn till dusk; drinking Slurpees; going to the beach (before
there was a South Beach); and having boatloads of fun without
a care in the world.

It was sometime during my childhood that I dreamed of becoming a medical doctor like my dad. My dad a very charismatic man in his youth, small in stature but loved by everyone he met. My mother, a very sociable, Christian woman, enjoyed entertaining and hosting fabulous events with organizations such as the Links, Jack and Jill, and her beloved sorority, Alpha Kappa Alpha Inc.

She was very pleasant with a quiet spirit, truly the backbone of our home during my childhood years. She made sure we attended Mount Sinai Baptist Church every Sunday, were in the best schools, and were taking classes that would challenge us academically.

I vividly recall when our family moved to a home with a pool in an upper-middle-class neighborhood; it was 1971. Miami Shores, still grappling with integration, inclusion, and cultural diversity, reluctantly accepted my sister and me into their neighborhood and schools. My dad would always tell us that the cream always rises to the top. In many ways, he knew the challenges we faced, and always encouraged us to do our very best.

Taking on my dad's persona, I quickly learned how to interact well with others and excel in the classroom. Instructors enjoyed teaching me, and I embraced learning from them. By the time I graduated from Miami Edison Senior High School, I was strong, confident, and self-assured, with my sights on attending one of the most prestigious historically black colleges of our generation: Morehouse College.

Morehouse College was established in 1867; its motto is *Et facta est lux*, meaning "And then there was light." It is an all-male African American liberal arts college known for cultivating great leaders such as Howard Thurman; Martin Luther King Jr.; Maynard Jackson; David Satcher, MD, PhD; Samuel Jackson; Spike Lee; Edwin Moses; Fernando Daniels, MD; Darryl Fortson, MD; Thomas Cox Jr., JD; Frank K. Jones, MD, MPH; Miles D. Johnson, MD; Kenyon Fort, DDS; Luther Burse, MD; Rod Amos, JD; Henry Thurston, MBA; Leonard Starks, PhD; Keith Allen, MD; Lieutenant Colonel Bruce Moody; Jonathan Pryor, MD, Captain, Medical Corps USNR; and William Kelvin Walker, MBA. It was led by presidents Benjamin E. Mays, Hugh Glosser, and Andrew Massey.

Morehouse believed in the philosophy of W. E. B. Dubois and the "Talented Tenth." As black men, we were the African American leadership class selected to lead the masses through our intellect. Dr. Dubois eloquently described this philosophy in his manuscript of the early twentieth century.

Forging a bond with like-minded men and pursuing our professional goals was paramount to my success while matriculating through the halls of Morehouse College, with its mystique and notoriety. Becoming a member of Omega Psi Phi fraternity (Psi chapter's Ly-On Nine), where our motto "Friendship is essential to the soul," is the essence of who I am as a man today.

Attending medical school would begin to shape and mold me professionally over the next thirty years. Medical school was also a time of my greatest heartache and pain. My mother became ill with colorectal cancer. Through all of her guidance, direction, and prayers, she admonished me to complete my assignment, although she would never live to see the fruit of her labor. Upon graduation from the University of Miami School of Medicine, I completed my internship and residency at Wayne State University Family Medicine program in Detroit, Michigan. It was there that I met my wife of twenty-three years and began a family of our own with three daughters Nia, Carin, and Amaya.

CHAPTER 1

Striving for Optimal Health

If you have raced with men on foot, and they have wearied you, how will you compete with horses? And if in a safe land you fall down, how will you do in the jungle of the Jordan?

—Jeremiah 12:5 (RSV)

WE ARE DESIGNED AT BIRTH to passionately pursue and achieve phenomenal things throughout our lives. We are equipped to pursue our dreams, hopes, and aspirations without reservations or doubt. Yet we continue to thirst for something so much more than what our society offers in the way of social media, celebrities, athletes, entertainers, politicians, and even clergymen. How do we, as mature, authentic members of society, prevent ourselves from short-circuiting our journey and neutralizing ourselves and our impact before we reach our destiny?

Surely theologians would say that we are created from the dust of the ground with a touch of divinity and that our creator desires a personal relationship with his created. Scientists would argue we are simply a compilation of molecular matter, existing as carbon molecules reacting with negative and positive ions in our environment. Philosophers would contend that we are physical beings in search of the meaning of life, constantly redefining our role with nature, each other, and our God.

Indeed, our challenge is to grow in excellence without becoming too self-absorbed, self-gratified, or self-promoted. We are given the task of serving others while not getting lost in ourselves. So often we are distracted or derailed by the unexpected in life—whether hurt feelings, broken promises, life's failures, loss of loved ones, loss of employment, wasted opportunities, illness, self-indulgence, or worse even still, too much power and authority over others.

When beset with mental, physical, or spiritual challenges, do we implode? Do we live cautiously or courageously? It is certainly easier to settle for mediocrity than to sustain the intestinal fortitude to transcend any obstacle, challenge, or controversy. Oftentimes throughout our journey, we are asked the question: Will we run with the horses and seek excellence in all thing we pursue? This implores the question: What is excellence? Excellence is a mindset, a state of being, that resonates with us as children or developed in us as adults over time through preparation, practice, and performance—whether we were in the classroom, preparing for final exams, or in the boardroom, preparing a multimillion-dollar proposal.

Whether you are a weekend athlete preparing for your first 5K run or a professional athlete at the pinnacle of your sport, excellence is an ongoing quest to be the best. Through discipline, desire, sterling examples, access, and attention to details, excellence becomes an integral part of who we are. Pursuing excellence means consistently making the right choices regarding our well-being. It means developing superb habits that would propel us toward our greatest achievements while we perform them automatically without hesitation. Over a lifetime, excellent choices assist us in establishing a foundation and identity that becomes second nature to who we are and what we desire.

So it is with optimal health and wellness—both essential components in achieving our goals. Interwoven in the pursuit for optimal health are our physical fitness, emotional vitality, environmental triggers, social values, spiritual beliefs, intellectual capacity, financial security, and occupational fulfillment. There is a delicate balance of energy that flows between our mind, body, and spirit as we strive for optimal health, wellness, and the pursuit of excellence.

We will explore several systems of the human body and the role that each system provides in achieving and sustaining optimal health. We will also review disease states that may compromise our journey.

CHAPTER 2

Optimizing Our Emotional Health

Emotion is created by a cause whether that cause
is factual, or imaginary does not matter, as long
as the believer holds it as true.

—Bangambiki Habyarimana, *Pearls of Eternity*

CRITICAL TO ACHIEVING OPTIMAL HEALTH is attaining emotional
wellness. Our passion for life is affirmed by a positive imagery that
is largely determined by our five senses (seeing, hearing, smelling,
touching, and tasting), connecting our external environment with
the innermost recesses of our mind. Can you imagine not being
able to visualize a sunset or fine art or imagine a world void of
classical music, jazz, country, hip-hop, rock, or gospel? Or imagine
not being able to smell the scent of a rose or the fragrance from
your favorite perfume or taste your mom's savory cooking or feel
the caresses and warmth of your loved ones? A world void of our

five senses is a lonely, dark world without the capacity to express the depths of our emotions on the canvas of our life.

———■———

Deep within the recesses of our mind is the emotional control center called the limbic system. A *well-developed*, highly functional limbic system's primary role is emotional vitality. It is composed of structures consisting of the thalamus, hypothalamus, amygdala, hippocampus, and cingulate gyrus.[1] Our emotional center receives external stimuli and information from neurosensory pathways that allow us to experience life at its best. Let's explore each structure closely to illustrate how our optimal health is intricately woven into our emotional well-being.

The thalamus: The thalamus's main function is to act as a relay and processing station for motor and sensory stimuli from our external environment to all areas of our brain. It plays a major role in the regulation of our awareness, thoughts, surroundings, and sleep. Injury to the thalamus may lead to a permanent vegetative state.

The hypothalamus: The hypothalamus receives information from the thalamus and initiates work within the pituitary pathways, which provide the delicate framework for influencing fight or flight, relaxation, hunger, sleep, and reproduction within our bodies.

---

1   Indian J Psychiatry. 2007 Apr-Jun:49(2): 132-139.

The amygdala: If the eyes are the windows to our soul, then the amygdala is the aperture to our emotions. Its main role is to assess fear, anger, and pleasure. Our innate survival instincts and the extent of our memory are drawn together by this small yet persuasive almond-shaped structure.

The hippocampus: Social discourse, the use and expression of language, and the adaptive ability to change are determined by the small curved formation in the medial temporal region of the brain called the hippocampus. Its primary role is memory, and *its* capacity for creativity, imagination, exploration, decision-making, and empathy allows the full expression of emotional wellness manifested through optimal health. Can you imagine a world without dreams, hopes, or imagination? Or a world devoid of peace, love, and kindness? It is our hippocampus, nurtured from birth with love, that produces great memories, possibilities, and potential.

The cingulate gyrus: The cingulate gyrus is located along the medial aspect of the cerebral cortex and acts as a portrait whose canvas displays the depths of our emotions, behaviors, and experiences that are established through neurocircuitry pathways. This portrait, set by each life experience, enhances the quality of our response to a range of emotions, including love, joy, peace, sadness, pain, and even fear. Our speech, understanding, and passion for all things we desire are crystallized under the healthy development of the cingulate gyrus.

Simply stated, the limbic system allows us to input, store, and respond to a range of emotions that permit us to gaze at our own image and realize how wonderful we really are.

———■———

Just as food nurtures and energizes our physical body, neurotransmitters fuel our mental and emotional well-being. Specifically, serotonin, dopamine, gamma-aminobutyric acid (GABA), and norepinephrine are all neurotransmitters designed to replenish the depth of our emotional passions expressed throughout our daily lives.

Serotonin: Serotonin is a neurochemical whose precursor is an amino acid called 5-hydroxytryptophan, which is pivotal to maintaining our limbic system's vitality. It has the ability to regulate mood, social behavior, appetite, and digestion.[2] There are several foods that naturally increase our tryptophan levels (the precursor to serotonin) and assist us in boosting our mood, withstanding the stressors of life, and enhancing our energy levels. Eggs, cheese, tofu, pineapple, nuts, seeds, salmon, and turkey are all excellent dietary sources for generating this mood-stabilizing neurochemical serotonin.[3]

---

2 MedicalNewsToday, "What is serotonin and what does it do?" Medically reviewed by Debra Rose Wilson, PhD, MSN, RN, on February 2, 2018. Written by James McIntosh (accessed September 28, 2019).
3 7 foods That Could Boost Your Serotonin: The Serotonin Diet; medically reviewed by Natalie Butler, RD, LD, on August 29, 2018. Written by Healthline Editorial Team (accessed September 28, 2019).

However, chronically elevated cortisol levels produced from adrenal stress, low blood glucose levels from poor dietary habits, and chronic inflammation from our muscles and joints rob the body of much needed tryptophan (the precursor to serotonin), which is paramount to our emotional well-being, sleep, hygiene, and vitality. There is currently ongoing medical research to quantify the impact serotonin produced in the gut has on the deep recesses of our mind. Let's delve into this connection between the gut and brain further.

Studies have shown that there is a perpetual molecular matrix between our brain and gut called the gut-brain axis. This pathway, composed mainly of our vagus nerve (the tenth cranial nerve in our central nervous system), allows our gut microbiome to produce serotonin. Serotonin continuously ascends and descends via this pathway to our limbic system.[4]

This network impacts our passions for life through the depths of our emotional expression and well-being. Have you ever had a pivotal presentation at work or school and developed a *queasy* stomach? Or ate a fulfilling meal and felt so relaxed and content? The gut-brain phenomenon is being stimulated and working on our behalf! This gut-brain connection is paramount in our pursuit of excellence in all things we desire. No wonder Thanksgiving dinner makes us feel so good!

---

4 Annals of Gastroenterology: The gut-brain axis: Interactions between enteric microbiota, central and enteric nervous systems. M. Carabotti, A. Scirocco. 2015-ncbi.nlm.nih.gov.

———

Dopamine: The neurotransmitter dopamine plays an equally vital role in risk versus reward, passions, movement, sleep, and memory. Many scholars classify this neurochemical as the happiness hormone. The anticipation of euphoria and keen pleasure surging from neurocircuitry pathways generated from the substantia nigra (an area of the brain that stores dopamine) are often manifested through this neurotransmitter. In addition, our executive function and decision-making are largely regulated by this neurohormone.

Dopamine is produced from the amino acids tyrosine and phenylalanine. Protein-rich foods such as turkey, lean beef, soy, legumes, and dairy are natural ways to enhance this hormone in our circulation. Even bananas, nuts, almonds, and dark chocolate stimulate tyrosine and phenylalanine production.[5] Throughout our lifetime, dopamine stimulates risk, daring, intrigue, and mystery. Whether we are mountain climbing, bungee jumping, or even skydiving, our substantia nigra supplies us with the thrill of the conquest. It can be an intoxicating desire that cannot easily be quenched.

Gamma-aminobutyric acid (GABA): On the other hand, our inhibitory neurotransmitter's primary role is to prevent overexcited neural synapses. Maintaining calm in the face of challenge and controversy is what this neurohormone helps us do best! This

---

5   Healthline, "How Does Dopamine Affect the Body?" Ann Pietrangelo. November 5, 2019.

hormone helps us from overreacting or becoming compulsive with our surroundings.[6]

Can you imagine being pushed to the edge—past the point of no return? Emotionally you are devastated, about to lose it all, when something out of anonymity speaks peace over your situation. GABA comes through in the form of a still, small voice. It calms the rage, admonishes the distraught, and comforts the brokenhearted until we are able to regroup mentally, physically, and spiritually, once again.

While there are no ordinary foods that naturally enhance GABA production, there are fruits, vegetables, teas, and red wines that may have a significant impact on GABA's availability in the brain.

The amino acids L-threonine and taurine are also precursors to this neuro-inhibitory transmitter. In addition, the minerals and nutrients magnesium, zinc, B6 (pyridoxal phosphate) and inositol are all essential elements in enhancing GABA within the limbic system.

There are several natural ways to boost GABA levels, and thus create feelings of calmness and relaxation. The herbal supplements valerian and ashwagandha help elevate GABA levels in the brain (by promoting production or slowing its breakdown). In addition, the *Journal of Biological Chemistry* suggests that breathing in the scent of jasmine may help enhance the effects of GABA.

---

6 Healthline, "What does Gamma Aminobutyric Acid (GABA) Do?" Medically reviewed by Dena Westphalen, PharmD, on October 26, 2018. Written by Healthline's Medical Network.

Norepinephrine: The neurotransmitter norepinephrine is responsible for anticipating and responding to stressful situations. It is the fight-or-flight hormone that gives us the strength to stand firm in the face of fear, meet our opponents face to face without hesitation, or sit at the table with our adversaries and not be afraid. In addition, adequate amounts of norepinephrine in our central nervous system allow individuals to avert depression and melancholy.

There are several foods that contain the amino acid tyrosine that naturally enhance norepinephrine supply. Bananas, beans, oatmeal, fish, lean meats, cheese, soybeans, and whole grains are just a few.[7]

Our emotional well-being plays such a major role in how we view the world and, more importantly, how we view ourselves. We are often faced with a multitude of challenges that test our aspirations, resolve, and ingenuity. Our emotional well-being often depends on our ability to face difficulties courageously, work through complex situations conscientiously, and persevere through hardship gallantly. If we are successful, we are able to elevate ourselves to another level of anticipation, hope, and desire.

In pursuit of excellence our ability to persevere through doubt, uncertainty, and insecurity, even in the face of rejection or exclusion, allows us to confront each difficulty or dilemma with confidence. Our destiny is shaped and molded by the ups and downs of life. As we continue to grow in wisdom and understanding

---

7 Natural Ways to Produce Norepinephrine. Addiction.com Staff on April 16, 2018, in Health Living.

through each season of life, our ability to interact compassionately with others as we embrace our potential and its transformative process is paramount to achieving optimal health and emotional wellness throughout our journey.

———■———

There is nothing more devastating or incapacitating to our emotional wellness than a stroke. Regardless of age, a stroke neutralizes our passions, disrupts our destiny, and alters the trajectory of our life's dreams, imagination, and creativity. The sudden loss of blood supply to our brain from a burst or blocked blood vessel not only impact the corresponding function of our body, but also our memories, decision-making, speech, behavior, understanding, and conceptual thinking are forever changed.

There are two major categories of strokes: ischemic and hemorrhagic. Eighty percent of all strokes are ischemic. This happens when blood flow to the brain is blocked by clots or the buildup of plaque. Hemorrhagic strokes occur from leaking vessels that interrupt the oxygen and nutrient flow to the brain. The amount of bleeding determines the severity of the stroke.

There are several risk factors that predispose individuals to a stroke:

- High blood pressure

- High blood cholesterol

- Atherosclerosis (plaque buildup in the blood vessel)

- Heart disease

- Adult onset diabetes

- Family history of stroke

- Previous transient ischemic attack (TIA)*

- Excessive weight

- Heavy alcohol consumption

- Cigarette smoking

- Inactive lifestyle

Most strokes have common warning signs and symptoms, such as the following:

- Sudden severe headache

- Dizziness or loss of balance

- Double vision or blurring in one or both eyes

- Weakening or numbness on one side of the body

- Difficult speaking or understanding others

- Confusion or difficult thinking

- Sudden loss of bowel or bladder control

The time it takes to recover from a stroke depends on the severity of damage to the brain. Regardless, early intervention is vital to preventing further damage and promoting long-term recovery. Diagnostic imaging test such as CT scans and MRIs are used to measure the extent and nature of the stroke. Rehabilitation often involves physical, speech, and occupational therapies. Recovery is usually a slow process that begins gradually over several weeks and continues for a year or more after the stroke.[8]

*Transient ischemic attack (TIA) is a temporary blockage of blood flow to the brain caused by small clots that dissolve shortly after lodging in vessel walls. Symptoms can last for a few minutes or up to twenty-four hours. TIAs are usually warning signs of an impending stroke and should be treated immediately.

---

8 Understanding Stroke; Scientific Publishing Ltd. Rolling Meadows USA #1455.

As we age, we will inevitably be challenged with the progressive memory loss (Alzheimer's type dementia) of our parents, friends, loved ones, or even ourselves. Studies have shown that there are currently five million cases out of forty-six million elderly in our population and growing. Alzheimer's is the fifth leading cause of death in individuals above sixty-five. Health-care costs are approaching $236 billion.

There are several factors that are known triggers:

1. Increased age

2. Family history

3. History of diabetes, stroke, and heart disease

4. Midlife obesity

5. Chronic use of certain medications

6. Lack of education

From a clinical perspective, onset is very gradual; patients often take longer to complete routine tasks, and it becomes difficult to perform tasks that require several steps to complete. There is also progressive forgetfulness (from the simple to the complex), from paying bills to daily hygiene.

As a clinician, it has been my experience that their greatest fear is losing their sense of independence and needing to rely on others for their normal activities of daily living (bathing, clothing, preparing meals, going to the restroom). Like most chronic disease clinicians confront, there is no cure for Alzheimer's disease (although medical research for the disease is very promising). However several factors reduce our risk and allow us to enjoy our senior years with enthusiasm.

1. Healthy lifestyle

2. Good dietary habits

3. Regular mental and physical activity

4. Maintaining an ideal body weight

5. Getting plenty of sleep

6. Minimizing alcohol use

7. Prescription free living

8. Taking a multivitamin daily

Hans Christian Andersen stated "Where words fail, music speaks". Research studies has shown that music can dramatically improve the mood of Alzheimer's patients. There is relatively strong evidence, with respect to music's ability to affect behavior, such as reducing anxiety and agitation. Scientific research shows that dementia sufferers who listen to music score better on test of thinking, memory, and learning.

Music therapist Connie Tomaino, executive director of the Institute for Music and Neurologic function in New York, observed patients in the dementia unit responded positively to music triggering and strengthening memory.[9] Researchers don't know why music therapy helps patients with dementia. Music might affect the brain in ways that are beyond the normal channels of intellectual processes that are damaged by dementia. It is possible that the brain processes music in ways that are closely linked to how memories are formed, stored, and recalled, a connection that might allow certain songs to unlock memories.[10] Although there is no cure for people with dementia, music can greatly enhance their quality of life.

9 Encyclopedia of Natural Health, Mental Health; pg. 48-50; Nick Tate. 2017
10 Ibid

CHAPTER 3

Optimal Gut Health

The road to health is paved with good intestines!

—Sherry A. Rogers

A MAJOR FACTOR IN ACHIEVING optimal health is our gastrointestinal system, which works synergistically with an abundance of natural, healthy gut bacteria to promote the digestion of carbohydrates, fats, and proteins. This system is paramount in providing our body the necessary fuel and energy it requires to pursue excellence in all things we desire.

The digestive process begins as soon as we begin to anticipate chewing food in our mouth; this triggers the release of an abundance of rich salivary enzymes called amylase, and this initiates the beginning of a transformative metabolic process of turning food into energy. Optimal stomach pH as well as gastric amylase produced by parietal cells is essential in catalyzing partially digested food particles into vitamins, minerals, amino acids, and nutrients for absorption. In preparation for absorption, the low pH of the stomach allows the emptying of partially digested food into the small intestines where digestive enzymes, bicarbonate, and bile acids are released from the pancreas and gall bladder. The release of these digestive enzymes and bile is triggered by a low pH in the stomach (an acidic environment). Without this acidic environment of the stomach, delayed gastric emptying, abdominal bloating, and fullness often develop. From the enzymatic processing of carbohydrates and proteins to the emulsification of fats, vast amounts of fuel are produced, stored, and delivered in an efficient manner to provide our entire system with energy at optimal levels for achieving our very best. The timely elimination of waste by the colon, triggered by high fiber, fruit, vegetables, and water, is also paramount to achieving healthy outcomes and reducing our risk of colorectal diseases.

—▬—

The digestive system's optimal conversion of carbohydrates, fats, and proteins into glucose, vitamins, minerals, and amino acids is the catalyst that fuels our mind, body, and spirit at peak performance for a lifetime. A dynamic, healthy gut flora is essential in creating a process of renewal and abundant energy for our well-being. Let's lean in and examine this process much closer.

There are literally trillions of normal gut bacteria designed to work synergistically with the gastrointestinal system to perform numerous functions. Included among these functions are:

1. Fueling our bodies with energy

2. Assisting in fighting off foreign invaders such as bacteria, viruses, and fungus

3. Producing nutrients designed to energize our body for peak performance

4. Providing precursors to neurochemicals that impact our sense of well-being and mood.

Our vast multicomplex human microbiome can be compared to an ecosystem whose microbial components are largely determined by our type of birth (natural versus C-section), diet, age, genetics, and even culture.[11]

This gastrointestinal ecosystem and its microbial components set the foundation that fuels our optimal health and well-being. The gut mucosal barrier (a protective group of cells that protect the external environment of the stomach from its internal environment where cellular activity occurs) is controlled by fine-tuned communications occurring between our gut microbiome (good bacteria) and our body's immune system. The balance between healthy and pathological situations (e.g., metabolic disorders) is crucial. This is under the tight influence of several factors

---

11   The Microbes of the Intestine: An Introduction to their Metabolic and Signaling Capabilities; W. Hsiao, PhD, C. Metz, PhD and J. Roth, MD: Endocrinology and metabolism clinics of North America. 2008.

including our genes, the foods we consume, and the medications or drugs we ingest.

In healthy situations, the composition of the gut microbiome is associated with a thicker protective mucus layer. This allows for the production of antimicrobial protection signals: short-chain fatty acids (such as butyrate and propionate). These short-chain fatty acids lead to a positive cascade of molecular reactions contributing to reduced food intake and improved glucose metabolism.[12]

In contrast, in unhealthy situations, changes in the gut microbiome are linked to several adverse reactions:

1. A depleted thin mucosal layer

2. Decreased antimicrobial defense

3. Reduced short-chain fatty acid production.[13]

This lowered sense of gut protection leads to a negative cascade of molecular events that results in the increased proliferation of bad bacteria (endotoxin Enterobacteriaceae). Altogether, these negative changes in the microbial environment and metabolites induce a leakage of toxic particles in the blood that leads to systemic inflammation, autoimmune reactions, food intolerance, nutrient malabsorption, and blood-brain barrier breach.

---

12 Ibid.
13 Ibid.

Many chronic medical conditions such as Alzheimer's dementia, Parkinson's, autism, depression, and multiple sclerosis, which adversely impact the central nervous system, are the end result of negative effects of an unhealthy microbiome (bad bacteria in the gut).[14]

———

Our gastrointestinal system is responsible for the digestion, absorption, and elimination of carbs, fats, and proteins; how can we sustain its optimal functioning for a lifetime as we pursue all things we desire?

The American diet is replete with refined carbs, saturated fats, and food additives, which have been linked to an increased risk of developing digestive disorders. Food additives contribute to increased gut inflammation, leading to a condition called increased intestinal permeability or leaky gut: "Saturated fats are associated with an increased risk of developing inflammatory bowel disease. Many processed foods contain artificial sweeteners, which may cause abdominal bloating and diarrhea. Several research studies suggest that artificial sweeteners may increase the number of bad gut bacteria that have been linked to irritable bowel syndrome (IBS), ulcerative colitis, and Crohn's disease. Therefore, eating a diet based on whole foods and limiting the

14 The Human Microbiota in Health and Disease. B. Wang: Engineering Volume3, Issue 1, February 2017, page 71–82.

intake of processed foods may be best for achieving optimal health through digestion."[15]

It's well known that fiber is beneficial for optimal digestion. Soluble fiber absorbs water and helps add bulk to your stool. Insoluble fiber helps your digestive tract keep everything moving along. Soluble fiber is found in oat bran, legumes, nuts, and seeds, while vegetables, whole grains, and wheat bran are good sources of insoluble fiber.

Prebiotics are another type of fiber that feeds your healthy gut bacteria that help reduce your risk of small intestinal bacterial overgrowth and inflammatory bowel conditions. Prebiotics are found in many fruits, vegetables, grains, and even apple cider vinegar. Hydration with water is essential to sustaining optimal health through digestion. Several studies recommend consuming 50 percent of your body weight in ounces to ensure adequate hydration. Constipation is the most common sign of a lack of adequate fluid hydration.

According to Healthline, another way to help meet your fluid intake needs is to consume fruits and vegetables that are high in water, such as cucumber, zucchini, celery, tomatoes, melons, strawberries, grapefruit, and peaches. There are also good fats containing omega-3 fatty acids such as nuts, flaxseed, and certain fatty fish (salmon, mackerel, and trout), which enhance absorption and help reduce inflammation of the digestive tract.[16]

---

15 Ibid.
16 10 Ways to Improve Your Gut Bacteria Based on Science-Healthline: R. Robertson, PhD; November 18, 2016

Stress reduction is vital in preventing chaos and sustaining peak performance through optimal digestive health. Unresolved stress may lead to stomach ulcers, irritable bowel syndrome, diarrhea, and even constipation. Stress management through meditation, exercise, and yoga has been shown to reduce the risk of inflammatory bowel disorders and enhance optimal digestive health.

Our digestive system is designed to provide an abundance of fuel and energy for our body's peak performance. However, smoking, excessive alcohol intake, and late-night eating can all be detrimental to its optimal functioning. At its best, our digestive system is the catalyst that energizes our mind, body, and spirit with vitamins, minerals, and nutrients to dream, imagine, and pursue excellence in all things we desire.

The most difficult time in my medical career was my sophomore year of medical school, after months of complaining of abdominal pain and spasms my mother developed copious amounts of dark blood mixed within her stool. (also known as hematochezia.) Her gastroenterologist confirmed my families worst suspicions, a large right sided colon mass that spread beyond the colon wall. After surgery, the surgical oncologist confirmed metastasis (spread of cancer to other organ systems) throughout her abdomen. The Bridges family went into crisis mode as we circled the wagons to support, love, and care for the woman who poured so much of herself into each of us. While she did not live to see my brother or myself graduate from medical school, she was able to glimpse from a distance the white coat (symbolic of all physicians) that I would wear as I transported her to chemotherapy.

Colon cancer screening is essential in ensuring we reach our utmost potential and destiny. Like most cancers, colon cancer is preventable. Colon cancer is the third most common cancer diagnosed in both men and women.[17] As of 2020 the American Cancer Society has reported 104,610 new cases of colon cancer each year, and 43,340 new cases of rectal cancer. [18]The United States Preventive Service Task Force recommends colon cancer screening at the age of 50 years and continue until age 75 years. For adults age 76 to 85 years, the decision to screen should be individualized. [19]

Risk factors for colon cancer are the following:

- Older age

- Minority race

- A personal history of colorectal cancer or polyps

17 American Cancer Society Guidelines for colorectal Cancer Screening, May 30, 2018
18 Ibid
19 www.uspreventiveservicestaskforce.org Screening for Colorectal Cancer Recommendatios USPSTF June 15.2016.

- Inflammatory Bowel conditions such as ulcerative colitis and Crohn's disease

- Inherited syndromes that increase colon cancer risk

- Family history of colon cancer

- Low fiber, high-fat diet.

- A sedentary lifestyle.

- Diabetes

- Obesity

- Smoking

- Alcohol

- Radiation therapy for cancer

———

Coping with Cancer: Most patients who are diagnosed with cancer, and without symptoms even when advanced react with optimism and hope. Patients with strong faith will often accept their diagnosis as the will of God and put trust on their religious faith to see them through the cancer. When initially diagnosed with cancer, the first step is to see a qualified specialist which is most often a medical or surgical oncologist. It is important to have a family member or close friend to accompany the patient to help ask questions and remember what is told. A second opinion is always helpful for reassurance and to help plan therapy. The most important factor in having the best outcome is sticking to the program. Cancer therapy can be very difficult with many side effects. Meditation, support groups, and helpful friends and family can contribute to a patient's success in undergoing treatment.[20]

---

20 Encyclopedia of Natural Healing, Cancer, pg.236;Nick Tate; 2017.

CHAPTER 4

Optimal Musculoskeletal Health

We are all sculptors and painters, and our material is our own flesh and blood and bones. Any nobleness begins at once to refine a man's features, any meanness or sensuality to imbrute them.

—Henry David Thoreau

MY WIFE AND I RECENTLY traveled to Florence, Italy, and had the opportunity to marvel at, among many things, the works of Michelangelo—specifically, his famous masterpiece and sculpture of David inside the Accademia Gallery Museum. From Michelangelo's vivid imagination and life's experiences, he sculpted a fifteen-foot youthful portrait of the future king of Israel. Strong hands, broad shoulders, and a chiseled chest and musculoskeletal system characterize this masterpiece. David stands poised and resolute as his eyes appear to be piercing through his target, Goliath.

Like Michelangelo's depiction of David, so is our amazing skeletal system, which contains 206 bones designed to provide protection, stimulate movement, store minerals, and promote blood production that supplies and sustains our well-being: "The framework of our skeletal system protects our vital organs (brain, lungs, heart, liver, stomach, and spleen) from blunt trauma or injury. Each bone, regardless of size, is strategically attached to muscles, tendons, and ligaments that are designed to reinforce, strengthen, and stabilize bony planes, which provide enhanced flexibility and a range of motion to our skeletal framework."[21]

A vital component to the mobility of each bony structure is cartilage. If our bones provide protection for our body, then cartilage provides the glue. The core components of this cartilaginous glue are cells called chondrocytes. These highly specialized cells produce an interwoven matrix of collagen, proteoglycans, and elastin fibers that bind firmly together to form the cornerstone of our skeletal system: "There are three types of cartilage based on the strategic placement, design, and function of each bone in the body. Hyaline cartilage, elastic cartilage, and fibrocartilage are all designed to provide a cushion for our bones, flexibility for our joints, and strength for our core."[22]

---

21 https://opentextbc.campus. Chapter 7.1 Divisions of the Skeletal System-Anatomy and Physiology
22 Ibid.

"Hyaline cartilage is translucent and most commonly found in the ribs, nose, larynx, and trachea. It is very firm, containing large amounts of collagen. Elastic cartilage is present in the outer ear, Eustachian tube, and epiglottis. It contains elastic fiber networks and collagen type II fibers. Its principal protein is elastin. Fibrocartilage is tough, strong tissue found predominantly in the intervertebral disks and at the insertions of ligaments and tendons; it is similar to other fibrous tissues but contains cartilage ground substance and chondrocytes. (the material that supports the growth of cells to cartilage)."[23]

All cartilage serves to enhance the skeletal system's ability to soar, peak, and thrive in our quest for a lifetime of optimal health. Musculoskeletal strength and fitness throughout our lifetime change the trajectory of our lives by allowing our joints the flexibility and mobility to achieve higher exercise goals, remain strong in the midst of aging, and steer clear from inactivity and chronic inflammatory conditions that seek to sideline our amazing journey.

We also must be very intentional and purposeful in our food consumption if we are to achieve and sustain optimal musculoskeletal support: "Whole grains, seafood, organic skinless poultry, eggs, soy or almond milk, leafy green vegetables, lentils, and legumes are all excellent sources of phytonutrients designed to fortify our skeletal framework for a lifetime. In addition, vitamins, nutrients, and minerals, such as calcium, magnesium, and vitamin

---

23 Ibid.

D3, are essential in supporting the intertrabecular network of our skeletal system. Eating an abundance of vegetables is paramount to our skeletal health."[24]

Cruciferous vegetables are one of the best sources of vitamin C, which stimulates the production of bone-forming cells: "Some studies even suggest that vitamin C's antioxidant effects may protect bone cells from damage."[25] In addition, engaging in specific types of exercise can help you build and maintain strong bones. One of the best types of activity for bone health is weight-bearing or high-impact exercise, which promotes the formation of new bone. It can also be extremely beneficial for preventing bone loss in older adults.

Strength-training exercise is not only beneficial for increasing muscle mass. It may also help protect against bone loss in older women. Getting enough dietary protein is important for healthy bones: "In fact, about 50 percent of bone is made of protein."[26]

"Researchers have reported that low protein intake impacts the intestinal absorption of calcium (the main mineral found in bone), affecting rates of bone formation and breakdown by stimulating the autoregulatory hormone of calcium, parathyroid hormone (PTH)."[27] "On the other hand, high-protein diets stimulate the production of insulin-like growth factors, which enhances

---

24 10 Natural Ways to Build Healthy Bones, Healthline: F. Spritzier, RD, CDE: January 18, 2017.

25 Ibid.

26 Protein, Calcium and Bone Density, G. Douglas Andersen, DC, Part 1, Dynamic Chiropractic, October 8, 2002 Vol. 20, Issue 21.

27 Low Protein Intake: The Impact on Calcium and Bone Homeostasis in Humans: J. E. Kerstetter et al. *J Nutr.* March 2003.

bone density, reduces the risk of fractures, and improves fracture recovery and repair after injury.[28] A low protein intake can lead to bone loss, while a high protein intake can help protect bone health during aging and weight loss.

Healthline has reported the basic recommendations for protein intake are 0.36 grams of protein per pound of body weight (0.8 grams per kilogram) daily. This translates to 56 grams of protein for a 154-pound (70-kilogram) individual.[29]

Calcium is the most important mineral for bone health, and it's the main mineral found in your bones. Because old bone cells are constantly broken down and replaced by new ones, it's important to consume calcium daily to protect bone structure and strength. The recommended daily intake (RDI) for calcium is 1,000 milligrams (mg) per day for most people, although teens need 1,300 mg, and older women require 1,200 mg. However, many people also need to supplement with up to 2,000 international units (IU) of vitamin D daily to maintain optimal levels.

To put things into perspective, while milk is a great source of calcium, there are several calcium rich foods, according to the National Osteoporosis Foundation:

---

28 Dietary protein is beneficial to bone health under conditions of adequate calcium intake: an update on clinical research; K. M. Mangano, 2014.
29 Protein Intake: How Much Protein Should You Eat Per Day? K. Gunnars, BSc. Healthline, July 5, 2018.

Produce	Serving Size	Estimated Calcium
Collard greens	1 cup	266 mg
Broccoli, fresh	1 cup	60 mg
Oranges	1 whole	55 mg
Salmon, canned	3 oz	180 mg
Shrimp, canned	3 oz	125 mg
Yogurt, low-fat	6 oz	310 mg
American cheese	1 oz	195 mg

A comprehensive guide to calcium-rich foods can be viewed at info@nof.org.

Vitamin K also supports bone health by modifying osteocalcin, a protein involved in bone formation. This modification enables osteocalcin to bind to minerals in bones and helps prevent the loss of calcium from bones.

Most vitamin K exists in small amounts in liver, eggs, and meat. Fermented foods like cheese, sauerkraut, and soybean also contain vitamin K, which assists in strengthening our bones. To build and maintain strong bones, follow a well-balanced diet that provides at least 1,200 calories per day. It should include plenty of protein and foods rich in vitamins and minerals that support bone health.

As we age, we can anticipate moderate amounts of bone and cartilage loss. However, researchers have shown there are several supplements designed to slow and even halt this process. In addition to calcium and vitamin D, glucosamine, chondroitin sulfate, methyl sulfonyl methionine, hyaluronic acid, and collagen are supplements designed to impact bone and cartilage loss. Turmeric (curcumin), a very popular spice for seasoning food, also assists in reducing inflammation of the musculoskeletal system. Boswellia extract, an herbal supplement, assists in reducing pain associated with degenerative changes of the skeletal system. All of these supplements in combination with healthy dietary habits and consistent exercise will allow many individuals to age with a sense of vigor, grace, and pizzazz.

Osteoarthritis versus rheumatoid arthritis: Arthritis involves joint damage that results in swelling, tenderness, stiffness, and loss of mobility. Osteoarthritis, also referred as degenerative joint disease, is the most common form of arthritis. It is characterized by a gradual loss of cartilage and overgrowth of bone from wear and tear or overuse. It primarily affects the spine, hips, knees, ankles, hands, and feet. On the other hand, rheumatoid arthritis is associated with one's own immune system attacking the lining of joints (synovial membranes), resulting in swelling, pain, stiffness, and decreased mobility.

Within each joint is articular cartilage designed to cover and protect the surface of the bone. In osteoarthritis, blunt trauma and stress can begin to erode the cartilage, resulting in cracks, cysts, and loose (osseocartilaginous) bodies within the joint space.

In rheumatoid arthritis an influx of inflammatory cells triggered by the immune system attacks the synovial membrane lining the joints, causing acute inflammation of the synovial membranes and initiating a progressive inflammatory process that leads to subcutaneous nodules, limited mobility, and bony erosions.

The most common symptoms of osteoarthritis are as follows:

1. Pain in a unilateral joint during or after use that is relieved by rest

2. Stiffness in a joint following inactivity that is relieved by movement

3. Crepitus (crackling sounds) during joint movement

4. Slow progression to constant, severe pain[30]

---

30 Scientific Publishing Ltd. Rolling Meadows, IL. USA #1050

Common symptoms of rheumatoid arthritis include the following:

1. Fatigue and weakness from systemic involvement

2. Joint pain, warmth, and tenderness

3. Joints affected in symmetrical pattern

4. Limited Joint mobility

5. Joint stiffness upon awakening and lasting longer than an hour

6. Subcutaneous nodules

7. Evidence of joint or bone erosion.[31]

Treatment of both osteoarthritis and rheumatoid arthritis involves daily exercise (balanced with rest), healthy eating habits, and the prevention of disability. Medications for both conditions are used cautiously and judiciously to mitigate symptoms and preserve a high quality of life.

Only as a last resort, when all other therapeutic options have failed, should surgery be considered to alleviate pain and suffering.

---

31   2005 Scientific Publishing Ltd., Rolling Meadows, Il. USA #1152

In osteoarthritis, inactivity is the biggest enemy to achieving optimal health. In rheumatoid arthritis, early detection and aggressive therapy are the keys to remission and pursuing excellence in all things you desire.

CHAPTER 5

Optimizing Our Renal Health

Bones can break, muscles can atrophy, glands can loaf, even the brain can go to sleep, without immediately endangering our survival, but when the kidneys fail to manufacture the proper kind of blood neither bone, muscle, gland nor brain can carry on.

—Homer William Smith

AS I COMPLETE THIS CHAPTER on optimizing renal health, I have just passed my first and hopefully last kidney stone. Oh my God! Forty-eight hours of pure hell. It began as I completed a very busy day of patient care in the world of family medicine; I worked through lunch while assisting my physician assistant on two minor in-office procedures. As our clinical staff completed their assignments for the day, I stayed back a few extra minutes preparing for the following day. After I went to the restroom, a wave of muscle spasm, tightness, sweating, and progressive excruciating pain over my left flank developed and lasted for the next forty-eight hours. Fortunately, I was less than five minutes away from the nearest emergency room. I called my best friend and confidante (my wife), who met me at the emergency room. She has been there with me, through it all, for the past twenty-five years. A renal CT scan confirmed a three-millimeter stone in the distal left ureter with mild hydronephrosis (swelling of the kidney due to an inability to properly drain urine from the kidney to the bladder). After receiving sufficient intravenous fluids, morphine, and Zofran, I was given the option of staying in the hospital or riding it out at home. Easy choice—or so I thought.

Kidney stones are a common urinary tract disorder that accounts for an annual cost of treatment estimated at $2.1 billion. The most common type of kidney stones contain calcium.

Risk factors for kidney stones include:

- a family history of stones

- recurrent urinary tract infections

- conditions affecting levels of calcium, phosphorus, and oxalate, substances in urine that foster kidney stone formation.

- Insufficient fluid intake

One of the best ways to prevent kidney stone formation is to drink two to three liters of fluid per day. Water is always best, but researchers have shown orange juice or lemonade to also be effective.[32]

———————

The role of any great facilitator is to extract the very best from each of the members in a group. With a unique skill set, the facilitator masterfully engages each member, then works with proficiency to attain the member's very best on behalf of the entire group. If there is any biological system within our human makeup that serves as a great facilitator, it is our renal system.

The renal system plays a crucial supporting role to every organ system in the human body. It consists of our kidneys, ureters, bladder, and urethra (in males, also the prostate). Oftentimes, it is glanced over until something goes awry with the elimination of waste, toxins, or chemical imbalances.

According to the National Kidney Foundation, twenty-six million Americans, about one in nine adults, have chronic kidney disease. This perpetuates an unfortunate need for dialysis and kidney transplant for individuals to stay alive. We cannot achieve optimal health and wellness without the keen awareness and efficiency of our renal system's ability to filter blood, secrete minerals,

---

32 Encyclopedia of Natural Healing; Kidney Stones: pg.388; Nick Tate; 2017

eliminate toxins, and reabsorb glucose, amino acids, and proteins in a timely fashion.

Let's explore the kidneys' vital role and function in assisting everything we attempt in the pursuit of excellence. Anatomically, the kidneys are located just below our lowest rib on each side of the spine. Each healthy kidney is four and a half inches long and weighs about five ounces. The infrastructure of each kidney is the functional unit called the nephron. Working at its best, each kidney has over one million nephrons. Each nephron has a ball of tiny capillaries called the glomerulus and a twisting tubule designed to work at maximal capacity.

As blood is filtered through the glomerulus into the tubule, the display of creative genius unfolds. Chemoreceptors and baro-receptors lining each tubule are able to detect the body's needs. From acid-base imbalance to volume regulation, each nephron secretes, reabsorbs, or eliminates efficiently and appropriately on behalf of the entire body.

The tubules join up to form the collecting system whose end results are the constituents of urine. Urine flows from the collecting system via the ureters to the bladder. The bladder stores urine until the time of voiding.

Our kidneys' surveillance of our body's molecular needs and its ability to meet those needs when healthy is phenomenal. From eliminating waste that our tissues and organs release into the blood (including creatinine, urea, nitrogen, and various toxic acids), to regulating our body's fluid balance, the renal system is working without cessation on our behalf.

In addition, the kidneys play a major role in the production of a hormone called renin that is designed to facilitate vasoconstriction of the arterial circulation in managing blood pressure. It also produces a hormone called erythropoietin, which stimulates the production of red blood cells by the bone marrow. Lastly, our kidneys facilitate the conversion of vitamin D to its biologically active form. This is very important for calcium absorption and maintaining the integrity of our skeletal system.[33]

Let's look a little closer at four very important parameters that reveal the health of our kidneys as we pursue excellence:

1. Blood urea nitrogen (BUN)

2. Creatinine

3. Estimated glomerular filtration rate (eGFR)

4. Urinalysis

Each is vital to assessing the health of our kidneys. When we consume a high-protein diet, nutrients are digested and absorbed through the intestinal mucosa. The end product of protein metabolism, ammonia, is transported to the liver and converted into urea and nitrogen, which are further eliminated through the kidneys.

---

33 Your Kidneys & How They Work niddk.nih.gov June 2018

Creatinine found in muscle fibers is metabolized through the kidneys. Serum creatinine is a nonspecific measure of assessing overall kidney function. The amount of blood that enters the kidney per milliliter per minute is known as the estimated glomerular filtration rate. It is the most sensitive indicator of kidney function. The stages of kidney disease are determined by the eGFR.

- Stage 1: eGFR is within normal range (greater than ninety) with protein in the urine or damage to the kidney.

- Stage 2: eGFR is in normal range (sixty to eighty-nine) with protein in the urine or mild damage to the kidney.

- Stage 3: eGFR is thirty to fifty-nine with moderate damage to kidney nephrons.

- Stage 4: eGFR is fifteen to twenty-nine with severe kidney damage to kidney nephrons.

- Stage 5: eGFR is less than fifteen. This is end stage renal disease, and renal dialysis is imminent.[34]

In order to sustain our kidneys for a lifetime, we must be aware of the various foods and liquids we consume. Maintaining this

---

34 Stages of Kidney Disease; www.davita.com

highly unique organ system skill set is paramount to achieving optimal health.

There are several foods that help maintain healthy kidney function. Salmon, spinach, onions, cabbage, sweet potatoes, garlic, olive oil, grapes, apples, strawberries, and blueberries are just a few foods rich in polyunsaturated fats that enhance kidney function.[35] Each food is designed to reduce inflammation, improve receptor sensitivity throughout the renal tubule, and enhance circulatory flow throughout the nephron. Preserving healthy kidneys (the great facilitators) through diet, hydration, exercise, smoking cessation, weight, and blood pressure management reduces the risk of chronic kidney disease.

———

As we age each year above forty, there is a precipitous decline in renal function. This renal decline is more pronounced in men than women. There are several factors that cause this decline. Research studies suggest advancing age, race, low socioeconomic status, or low educational levels are leading causes of renal decline. Poorly controlled diabetes mellitus and hypertension are equally as detrimental to kidney health. They are the two leading causes of end stage renal disease leading to dialysis.

There are several clinical signs of kidney disease that do not usually occur until late in the disease process:

_____
35 Medical News Today; What foods are good for kidneys? Medically reviewed by K. Marengo LDN,R.D. June 5, 2019,Written by Jon Johnson

These manifestations include the following:

1. Swelling around the eyes or legs

2. Fatigue

3. Drowsiness

4. Brain fog

5. Nausea/vomiting

6. Shortness of breath

7. Ashen skin (called "uremic frost")

8. Urinelike odor to the breath

9. Numbness and tingling in the hands or feet

10. Involuntary limb movements

11. Sleep disorders

12. Itching

13. Muscle cramps

14. Anemia of chronic disease[36]

These symptoms may be associated with other disease states that also are a contributing factor in kidney failure.

If it is inevitable that our renal system will decline slowly as we get older, we must learn to embrace every opportunity and assignment that allows us to reposition ourselves for growth and excellence. We must embrace a plant-based diet (instead of an animal-based diet), emphasizing cruciferous vegetables, fresh fruit, and whole grains to assist in preserving kidney function. Without exception, copious amounts of water also maintain kidney endurance and vitality, preventing the accumulation of various toxins throughout the entire system.

Our kidneys are amazing facilitators working on our behalf behind the scenes and keeping our bodies' complex physiologic system in harmony; they are always evolving, assisting, and supporting all our pursuits and endeavors.

It's so important that we preserve our kidneys through healthy dietary and lifestyle choices. If we do not, we may risk short-circuiting these great facilitators and our potential for excellence.

Diabetes mellitus is such an insidious formidable foe to our kidneys, optimal health and wellness. Once an individual develops

---

36 National Kidney Foundation; About Chronic Kidney Disease: Symptoms and causes, kidney.org

symptoms of urinary frequency, excessive thirst, weight loss, fatigue, blurred vision, recurrent skin infections, and complications of vascular disease and nerve damage the pancreas (the organ that produces insulin in response to elevated glucose levels from a carbohydrate meal) has lost half of its ability to produce insulin. However, when the interaction of glucose and insulin are maintained we are able to achieve and sustain excellence in all our desires.

A chronic imbalance in blood glucose (sugar) levels leads to diabetes mellitus. Type one diabetes mellitus occurs when there is complete failure of the pancreas to produce insulin. This is usually caused by an autoimmune process. (Our immune system attacks and destroys the beta cells within the pancreas that produce insulin.) This condition is often diagnosed in childhood. On the other hand, type two diabetes occurs when the body resist insulin or when there is not enough insulin produced by the pancreas to meet the high glucose demand. The lack of sufficient insulin prevents glucose from entering cells, so the body is not fully energized to pursue excellence. Type two diabetes is usually diagnosed later in life.

Let's unravel the mystery of what many of our ancestors called "Sugar". After a meal a cascade of metabolic events occur.

- Our digestive system metabolizes carbohydrates to glucose.

- Glucose enters the bloodstream.

- The pancreas responds to a rise in blood glucose by producing insulin into the bloodstream.

- Insulin stimulates cells to take up glucose and use glucose as fuel for energy.

- Insulin suppresses glucose production in the liver and signals the liver to increase glucose uptake to store for times of starvation or a missed meal.

As a result of insulin action in the blood stream, glucose levels fall, insulin production ceases, and balance in the body is restored. If individuals do not eat for more than four hours your body starts to run low on its immediate glucose supply and several metabolic events occur.

- Diminished blood sugar can deplete your energy and make you feel very weak.

- Low glucose can also make it hard to concentrate because your brain does not have the fuel it needs to function properly.

- The pancreas responds to low blood glucose levels by producing a hormone called glucagon into the bloodstream.

- Glucagon stimulates the liver to release glycogen (the stored form of glucose) into the bloodstream.

- As blood glucose levels rise, glucagon production ceases and balance in the body is again restored.

As long as this glucose balance between insulin and glucagon are maintained throughout our circulation, we are poised to pursue excellence in all things we desire.

———————

When diabetes mellitus gets dangerously out of control it can lead to end organ damage and devastating consequences.

- Visual disturbances leading to blindness

- Kidney failure leading to end-stage kidney disease and renal dialysis.

- Atherosclerosis (hardening of the arteries leading to heart disease.)

- Peripheral Neuropathy (Numbness and tingling of extremities leading to severe nerve damage).

While diabetes is a chronic progressive disease successful treatment and management includes

- a healthy lifestyle

- consistent exercise

- stress management

- proper sleep hygiene

- compliance with medication.

A few successful tips can lead to a long healthy life:

- Monitor blood glucose levels and your hemoglobinA1c. (Three month measure of glucose status in the blood)

- Eat regularly and do not skip meals.

- Choose well balanced foods. (High fiber with vegetables, fruit, and protein.)

- Avoid sweets and high fat foods.

- Limit or avoid alcohol

- Exercise regularly

- Maintain ideal body weight

- Take medication as prescribed.

CHAPTER 6

Optimal Heart Health

Above all else, guard your heart, for it is the well-spring of life.

—Proverbs 4:23 (NIV)

A SEVENTY-EIGHT-YEAR-OLD FEMALE PATIENT PRESENTED with a six-week history of progressive shortness of breath and fatigue while preparing her breakfast and performing household chores; she subsequently called her daughter, who scheduled an appointment with my office. Upon further questioning, a past medical history of diabetes mellitus, hypertension, hyperlipidemia, and mild obesity with a body mass index (BMI) of thirty-two was noted. She was compliant with her daily regimen of seven medications.

As I began her examination, I observed an elevated blood pressure, prominent jugular veins pulsating along the right side of her neck, a heart murmur, lung crackles (fluid in the lungs noted when listening with a stethoscope), and both legs swelling.

An electrocardiogram followed by an echocardiogram and cardiology referral confirmed my suspicions of congestive heart failure.

———

Over a lifetime the heart pumps a steady flow of oxygen, nutrients, hormones, and immune fighting cells to every organ system in our body. This magnificent four-chambered muscular organ, about the size of one's fist, is located between the lungs to the left of the chest. The heart has the ability to pump blood throughout the venous and arterial circulation of our body. At its best, our heart is a dual pump system that allows a venous flow of carbon-dioxide-rich blood to the right side of the heart while an arterial flow of oxygen-rich blood circulates from the lungs to the left side of the heart.

Oxygen-rich blood travels throughout the entire body, delivering oxygen, nutrients, and fuel to every cell, tissue, and organ for optimal utilization and health. As our heart is equipped to supply our entire body with oxygen-rich nutrients, it must also nurture itself through patent coronary vessels designed to ensure adequate cardiac muscle contractility and perfusion of blood through each chamber of the heart.

As blood flows through each chamber of the heart, there are two pairs of heart valves that regulate flow: the atrioventricular valves and the semilunar valves. The atrioventricular valves divide the upper atrium from the lower ventricles, preventing the return of blood flow into the atrium during contraction (or systole).

Likewise, the semilunar valves located along the base of the pulmonic and aortic trunk prevent the backflow of blood into the ventricles during relaxation (or diastole). Each beat of our heart is triggered by the closure of our atrioventricular ("lub") and semilunar ("dub") valves. These heart sounds are manifestations of the rhythm and flow of each cardiac cycle. The electrical rhythm of our heart originates along the sinoatrial node located along the right atrium or upper chamber. Electrical impulses diffuse across the atrium (causing contraction) to reach the atrial ventricular node; there is a slight pause before electrical impulses spread down the Purkinje fibers of the ventricles, causing contraction.[37]

There are several ways to keep our heart working at its best for a lifetime. Through a healthy diet, regular exercise, stress management, and proper sleep hygiene, we can equip ourselves to pursue, achieve, and sustain excellence in all things.

Transformative sustainable change always begins with the heart. It must begin with the choices we make to create an environment to propel us toward excellence. We must remain tenacious in our desires to incline our hearts toward excellence when combating distractions seeking to steal our authority.

Whether threats of gluttony, a sedentary lifestyle, procrastination, classism, racism, or bullying seek to derail us, we must

---

37 How the Heart Works; nhlbi.nih.gov

constantly reposition and reset our hearts as we evolve into all we desire. Challenges we face while pursuing excellence will inevitably come. We must know where to abide, renew our strength, and protect our heart. Remaining steadfast, with active anticipation and a healthy heart, allows our continued pursuit of excellence.

———■———

Our society has an obsession with obtaining everything instantly—from fast cars and planes to fast women and men to fast food. We have become obsessed with having it our way now. Most individuals are addicted to microwaved, processed, supersized, fried, fatty, and greasy foods as well as sugary beverages. Is there any wonder why heart disease remains the number one cause of our untimely demise? We can and must eat healthier. The American Heart Association has endorsed the Mediterranean diet as a way of obtaining a healthier heart lifestyle that will sustain optimal health for a lifetime. This is a meal plan rich in whole grains, fruits, and vegetables. This meal plan includes very minimal red meat and skinless poultry and an abundance of seafood. While these foods may not be the most popular at the family reunion or social gathering, they are by far the healthiest!

When I am discussing the Mediterranean meal plan with my patients and asking them to consider healthier eating. I will often use the atherosclerotic cardiovascular disease (ASCVD) risk estimator as a powerful tool to encourage compliance. It gives each patient a ten-year and lifetime risk of having a cardiovascular event. It also provides very practical recommendations to reduce your current risk.

In addition to healthy eating, consistent exercise is important. The American Heart Association and US Department of Health and Human Resources endorse 150 minutes of moderate activity or 75 minutes of vigorous activity per week.[38] This includes brisk walking, cycling, jogging, playing tennis, swimming, and even weight-bearing activity. The key is remaining vibrant and fit for a lifetime to reduce our risk for cardiovascular disease or an early death.

———■———

The American Heart Association has defined Life's Simple 7.[39] These are tools to enhance our cardiovascular health by improving seven risk factors in our daily lives.

1. **Managing blood pressure.** A normal blood pressure as defined by the Eighth Joint National Committee (JNC 8) is 120/80. Any blood pressure consistently above 135/85 is considered hypertensive. Most of us love well-seasoned food; however, excessive salt intake, caffeine consumption, and fried foods are major dietary triggers that lead to elevated blood pressures. In addition, a family history of high blood pressure, a sedentary lifestyle, and obesity are

---

38 How much physical activity do you need? Heart.org
39 American Heart Association, Life's Simple 7.

also major factors that may increase your risk of developing hypertension.

2. **Controlling cholesterol.** Persistently elevated cholesterol in the blood leads to plaque forming on the blood vessel walls that may impede blood flow, resulting in heart disease and strokes. To reduce this risk, healthy values for total cholesterol should be less than two hundred. High density lipoprotein (HDL) or good cholesterol removes excessive cholesterol from the circulation before it is able to form plaque on the blood vessel wall. HDL values should be greater than 40. Low density lipoprotein (LDL) or bad cholesterol transports excess cholesterol from the liver into circulation. LDL values should be less than 100. Triglycerides are indicative of daily fatty food consumption. These levels should be less than 150.

3. **Reducing blood sugar.** Low glycemic index foods are a great way to reduce daily glucose levels and reduce your risk of developing diabetes mellitus. An example of low glycemic index foods is carbohydrates that are slowly digested and absorbed, causing a slower and smaller rise in blood sugar levels. High glycemic index foods are quickly digested and absorbed, causing a rapid rise and fall of blood sugar levels. Examples of low glycemic index foods are whole wheat bread, oatmeal, oat bran, sweet potato, corn, lima/butter beans, peas, carrots, legumes, lentils,

most fruits, and non-starchy vegetables. The hemoglobin A1c is a diagnostic tool to measure how well controlled or how poorly controlled your blood glucose levels have been over the past ninety days. Hemoglobin A1c normal levels are 4.8–5.6. Prediabetic levels are 5.7–6.4. Diabetic levels are greater than 6.4.

4. **Active living.** Increased physical activity is one key to a longer, healthier life. The American Heart Association recommends walking ten thousand steps daily. This helps to lower cholesterol and blood pressure, improve energy and stamina, and enhance weight loss.

5. **Eating better.** The Mediterranean meal plan, which is full of grains, fruits, and fresh vegetables, is a great place to begin a longer, healthier way of life.

6. **Losing weight.** Most individuals have the ability to lose weight. Our challenge is to sustain the weight loss achieved. One key component in sustaining weight loss is monitoring caloric consumption. For example, if a 250-pound man is interested in losing 35 pounds and maintaining a daily weight of 215 pounds, he must understand that in order to lose one pound per week, he must reduce his caloric consumption by 3,500 calories per week, or 500 calories per day. A 2,000-calorie meal plan will allow him to reach

his goal naturally in six to nine months (depending on his overall health and level of physical activity).

7. **Quitting smoking.** Smoking, in all of its forms (cigarettes, cigars, weed, vaping) is kryptonite to a healthy lifestyle. The dangers of smoking have been well researched and documented. Research from the American Lung Association reveals that cigarette smoke contains more than seven thousand chemicals, at least sixty-nine of which are known to cause cancer. Even among smokers who have quit, chronic lung disease still accounts for 50 percent of smoking-related conditions. Smoking harms nearly every organ in the body and is a main cause of lung cancer and chronic obstructive pulmonary disease. Likewise, smoking leads to esophageal cancer by damaging the structure of cells that line the inside of the esophagus. It also leads to stomach cancer (due to repeated Helicobacter infection) and chronic progressive gastric ulcer formation. Additionally, dipping tobacco causes oral cancer. Even bladder cancer is very prominent among smokers. For all these reasons and more, smoking should not be a part of who we are or want to become. Cancer prevention trumps cancer treatment. Founder and CEO of the Prevent Cancer Foundation says If people did everything we know about preventing cancer, ideally, we could eliminate half of cancer incidence and prevent half of cancer deaths[40].

40 Encyclopedia of Natural Healing: Cancer pg24; Nick Tate. 2017

These seven measures have one unique thing in common: healthier outcomes! Reducing our risk of chronic illness or an early death is paramount. In pursuing excellence, we all must commit ourselves to a long, productive healthy lifestyle.

Yet stress from children, finances, school, relationships, and even employment impacts every aspect of our lives. Researchers have shown that stress stimulates the adrenal gland to produce the endorphin adrenaline that triggers the fight-or-flight response stimulated by the sympathetic nervous system. Likewise, cortisol, also produced by the adrenal gland and accurately depicted as the stress hormone, acutely allows us to accomplish phenomenal things but chronically can adversely impact every system in our body. Cortisol's long-term impact on our cardiovascular system is manifested as vasoconstriction of our coronary and peripheral blood vessels that may precipitate chest pain and elevations in our blood pressure. Everyone feels stress and reacts to it in different ways. How much stress you experience and how you react to it can lead to a wide variety of health problems.

"When stress is excessive, it can contribute to everything from high blood pressure, to asthma to ulcers to irritable bowel syndrome," said Ernesto L. Schiffrin, MD, PhD, physician-in-chief at the Jewish General Hospital and professor and vice chair of research for the Department of Medicine at McGill University in Montreal.[41] Stress may affect behaviors and factors that increase heart disease risk. Some people may choose to drink too much

41 Stress and Heart Health/ Alliance Work Partners Feb 12, 2019 E.L. Schiffrin, M.D., Ph.D.

alcohol or smoke cigarettes to "manage" their chronic stress; however these habits can increase blood pressure and may also damage artery walls.

Your body's response to stress may be a headache, backache, or stomachache. Stress can reduce your energy and sleep and make you feel agitated, forgetful, and out of control. A stressful situation sets off a chain of events. Your body releases adrenaline, a hormone that temporarily causes your breathing and heart rate to speed up and your blood pressure to rise. These reactions prepare you to deal with the situation—the fight-or-flight response. When stress is constant, your body remains in high gear off and on for days or weeks at a time. This can lead to damage to the vascular circulation.

Can managing stress reduce or prevent heart disease? Managing stress is a good idea for your overall health, and researchers are currently studying whether managing stress is effective for preventing heart disease. A few studies have examined how well treatment or therapies work in reducing the effects of stress on cardiovascular disease. Studies using psychosocial therapies in conjunction with medical therapy to reduce depression, anxiety, and stress are promising in the prevention of second heart attacks.

After a heart attack or stroke, people who feel depressed, anxious, or overwhelmed by stress should talk to their doctor or other health care professionals. According to a 2007 study, incorporating the foods and eating habits of the Mediterranean meal plan can reduce your risk for heart disease.

A comprehensive, healthy Mediterranean meal plan includes the following:

1. An abundance of antioxidant rich fruits and vegetables

2. Whole grains, beans, nuts (one handful per day), and seeds

3. The use of healthy, monounsaturated fats such as olive and canola oils

4. Moderate amounts of lean protein, fish, and eggs

5. A very small amount of red meat

Exercising for a healthy heart includes the following activities:

1. Resistance training for twenty minutes, three to five days a week

2. Staying hydrated (especially drinking plenty of water before, during, and after exercise)

3. Exercising with a family member, friend, or group to remain motivated and committed

4. Brisk walking, riding a bike, or swimming (for beginners 10 minutes working up to 30 minutes.)[42]

We must begin to change our thinking as it relates to food. Do we live to eat, or eat to live? Research has shown that ninety-five percent of heart related deaths are preventable with dietary changes. Reducing our consumption of bread, refined carbohydrates, and limiting animal products like red meat, pork, eggs, and chicken and consuming a diet rich in natural plant-based foods like vegetables with an array of colors filled with phytonutrients would significantly reduce our risk of developing heart disease.

Proper sleep hygiene is also vital to a healthy heart: The National Sleep Foundation has recommended seven to nine hours of restful sleep each night, regardless of age, weight, sex, or comorbidities (the presence of two or more chronic diseases in a patient). Studies have shown that our body chemistry requires adequate amounts of rest each day to support glucose metabolism, blood pressure, and the regulation and reduction of inflammation that may otherwise lead to plaque buildup, resulting in atherosclerosis and coronary artery disease.

There are several natural ways to get a good night sleep without the adverse effects of prescription medication.

- Chamomile tea. This soothing drink has a calming effect that relaxes the body in preparation for sleep.

---

42 https://www.diabetesalaska.com; Mediterranean Diet-Diabetes and Lipids Clinic of Alaska.

- Valerian root. This medicinal plant is a powerful sedative and anxiety reducer that helps individuals fall asleep faster and sleep more deeply than pills.

- Magnesium. Research studies show small deficiencies in this element can prevent the body from calming down at night.

- Zinc. Studies have shown that zinc supplements are natural sleep aids.

Proper sleep hygiene is essential to a good night of sleep. This includes:

- Changing your diet. Eating earlier and lighter in the evening improves sleep.

- Eliminating excessive alcohol, caffeine, or sugar in the evening improves sleep.

- Exercise early in the day. Endorphins released during exercise may make it difficult to sleep in the evening.

- Settle down before bedtime. Meditation, and calming music help prepare the mind and body for sleep.

- Make your bedroom a sanctuary. Reserve your bed for sleep and intimacy only.

- Keep a regular schedule: Go to bed at the same time each day.

- Take only short naps. Avoid long naps that can make it more difficult to sleep at night.

- Beware of "blue light". Electronic devices at bedtime disrupt sleep because of their ability to produce a blue light that is equivalent to sunlight.[43]

———■———

There are several characteristics of a healthy heart that will sustain us in our pursuit of excellence:

- A healthy heart desires healthy living.

- A healthy heart seeks to understand healthy outcomes.

- A healthy heart trusts the process to achieve a healthy lifestyle.

---

43 Encyclopedia of Natural Healing, sleep disorders pg. 432-433. Nick Tate: 2017

- A healthy heart seeks unity, wholeness, and truth in all things.

- A healthy heart seeks strength to bear good fruit in all seasons of life.

- A healthy heart creates habits that sustain excellence in all things.

- A healthy heart is a hopeful heart seeking to stay in the rhythm and flow of life.

CHAPTER 7

Optimizing Each Breath

Then the LORD God formed man of dust from the
ground and breathed into his nostrils the breath
of life; and man became a living being.

—Genesis 2:7 (RSV)

AN ANONYMOUS POET ELOQUENTLY WROTE, "Life is not mea-
sured by the number of breaths that we take, but by the moments
that take our breath away."

If there is one involuntary activity we as humans take for
granted and simply cannot live without, it is breathing. Let's look
closely at this phenomenon that fuels every aspect of our mind,
body, and spirit. We all require oxygen circulating through our
body to metabolize nutrients and release the energy we need to
achieve optimal health.

Our respiratory system provides us with oxygen from our external environment and expels carbon dioxide. It is actually the

interaction of carbon molecules that is essential to our biochemical composition and innate survival.

During a complete cycle of breathing (which includes inspiration and expiration), our diaphragm is lowered during contraction, the muscles between our ribs (intercostal muscles) lift our chest cavity upward, the volume of our chest cavity expands, a vacuum is created by additional space, and oxygen is drawn into our body.

During expiration, the muscles between our ribs relax, the chest cavity contracts, the lungs passively recoil, and carbon dioxide is pushed out of our lungs into the atmosphere. This seemingly simple involuntary act initiates a pathway that ends in the molecular gas exchange that is the catalyst that fuels every cell of our being.[44]

Let's continue to unveil this respiratory sequence that fuels and ignites our peak performance. As we inhale, oxygen enters through our nasal cavity or mouth and flows through our throat, voice box, and windpipe (trachea) into our right and left bronchi. Each lung transports oxygen into smaller tubes called bronchioles that finally reach their next destination: balloon sacs called alveoli.

There are over four hundred million alveoli formed within the innermost recesses of the lungs. The alveoli are responsible for molecular gas exchange. Blood is carried to tiny capillaries that wrap around each alveolus. Oxygen diffuses across the alveolar

---

44 Physiology of breathing-https://opentextbc.ca>chapter.22.3

wall into the blood as carbon dioxide diffuses from the blood into the alveoli. Newly oxygenated blood is transported from the lungs to the heart before circulating to the entire body. This perpetual respiratory phenomenon fuels and ignites our bodies' peak performance for a lifetime. Even still, our lung function does declines with age, like the function of other parts of our body.

Several factors impact our lungs functioning at their best.

1. Aging: According to the American Lung Association, lungs mature by the age of twenty-five; after age thirty-five lung function begins to gradually decline. This is primarily caused by a decrease in the function of the diaphragm as well as a loss of elasticity of the lungs.

2. Smoking: According to the American Lung Association, smoking is the leading cause of preventable deaths in the United States, causing 480,000 deaths per year. Secondhand smoke causes 41,000 deaths per year.

3. Exposure to air pollution: Ozone (smog) and particle (exhaust fume) pollutants may cause low birth weight and premature death, as well as harmful lung conditions (asthma attacks, bronchitis, and lung cancer) that may shorten the lifespan of children and adults.

4. Repeated respiratory infections: Chronic illnesses that weaken the immune system increase the risk of

repeated respiratory infections such as respiratory syncy-
tial virus (RSV) and pneumococcal infections.

5. Bone loss: Osteoporosis-induced fractures leading to
    kyphosis (outward curvature of the spine) and vertebral
    compression fractures may impair lung function.

6. Obesity: Obesity compresses the diaphragm and chest cav-
    ity, leading to a restrictive pulmonary system and impaired
    lung function. These factors all impact peak performance
    of the lungs and our ability to take a deep breath.[45]

The case of acute respiratory failure that I remember so vividly
as a clinician is of a male smoker who was incarcerated for over
twenty-five years and allergic to most environmental allergens
from dust mites, mold, ragweed, and a variety of grasses. Upon his
release from prison, he unsuccessfully attempted to cease smoking several times; in his personal life, he rekindled the flames
of love and married his high school sweetheart. Within the first
six months of marriage, one early morning he succumbed to an
anaphylactic reaction resulting in acute respiratory failure, while
his EpiPen and ashtray were both on his nightstand.

How can we keep our lungs functioning at an optimal level
as we age? How do we prevent ourselves from developing chronic
obstructive pulmonary disease, pneumonia, or even lung cancer?

45 American Lung Association/ Tips to keep your Lungs Healthy/ March
11, 2020

1. **Eating more fruit.** A study in the December 1, 2017, *European Respiratory Journal* found that a higher intake of antioxidant- and flavonoid-rich fruits, like bananas, apples, and tomatoes (about four servings of fruit per day) was associated with a slower decline in lung function, especially among ex-smokers.[46]

2. **Doing core and upper-body training.** Regular weight training can increase bone strength, and exercises like chest and shoulder presses and dead lifts can strengthen the chest, shoulders, and back muscles. This can help you maintain a breathing-friendly posture and take full breaths.

3. **Performing exercise resistance.** Aerobic exercise can help improve lung capacity—the amount of oxygen you take in with each breath. Try to include some resistance workouts in your regular routines. For instance, add some hills to your daily walks or walk while holding light hand weights or use the interval or random setting when on the treadmill. "These steps increase the intensity and variability of your workouts," says Dr. Waxman. "That raises your heart rate and makes you breathe harder, which ultimately can help improve lung capacity."[47]

---

46 Dietary antioxidants and 10 year lung function decline in adults-European Respiratory Journal by V Garcia-Larsen 2017 50: 1602286
47 Breathing life into Your Lungs-Harvard Health, April 1, 2018

4. **Getting vaccinated.** Getting vaccinated helps to prevent repeated respiratory infections like pneumonia. In addition to getting an annual flu vaccine, there are two kinds of pneumonia vaccines: Prevnar 13 (PCV13) and Pneumovax 23 (PPSV23). The Centers for Disease Control (CDC) recommends both vaccines for adults ages sixty-five and older. You should receive a dose of PCV13 first, followed by a dose of PPSV23 at least a year later.

5. **Practicing proper breathing.** Being aware of our breathing patterns helps us control deep physical and psychological challenges we face during our lifetime. With every aspect of our being, we must learn to breathe life into our passions, pursuits, hopes, dreams, and imaginations. Breathing new life into our situation allows space between our current pace and actual limits. Continued living on the edge of life leaves no room for the unexpected in life, whether personal, professional, or financial. Living on the edge, forfeiting peace for prosperity and fame, often takes years off your life leaving you lonely and dejected. Breathing new life means maximizing each twenty-four hours given and trusting the process of renewal and restoration of our mind, heart, and spirit. Being able to give your best each and every day in all areas of your life. Realizing that everything is made beautiful in time. Breathing new life into our existence means embracing joy instead of sorrow, peace instead of chaos, hope instead

of despair, love instead of hate. We are a composite of the choices we make and the experiences we encounter along our journey. Breathing new life signifies understanding how finite our lives actually are while embracing wisdom with each breath we take. Each impactful decision we make allows us to leave a lasting legacy of enduring peace and stability.

A man of many words, my father-in-law, Mr. Will Webster, knew the value of the saying "Whatever is has already been, and what will be has been before, and God will call the past to account." Originally from Jackson, Mississippi, he would often tell me, "Lloyd, don't stress about that sugar-honey iced tea. It is what it is, and it's going to be exactly how it's going to be."

There are several benefits of performing deep breathing exercises throughout the day:

1. Increasing the positive energy level in the body and helping remove toxins

2. Helping supply more oxygen to the body

3. Enhancing blood circulation throughout the body

4. Reducing heart-related problems

5. Increasing focus and concentration

6. Shifting the autonomic nervous system from the fight-or-flight sympathetic system to the calming parasympathetic state.

7. Relaxes the mind and the body[48]

—▬—

Measuring Lung Function: Assessing lung function and response to therapy is vital in managing acute and chronic lung conditions. Spirometry is the most common type of breathing test. This test measures how much air you can breathe in and out of your lungs, as well as how easily and fast you can blow the air out of your lungs. This simple test provides vital information on the health of your lungs and is an excellent prognostic tool that is widely used in primary care settings.

There are two very common respiratory conditions that are worthy of distinction: chronic obstructive pulmonary disease and asthma. Chronic obstructive pulmonary disease (COPD) is characterized by a progressive inflammation of the bronchial lumen and destruction of the bronchial tree and airway sacs, which make it very difficult to breath over time. The most common cause of COPD is cigarette smoking. However, there is also a genetic component called alpha-1 antitrypsin deficiency.

---

48 Health Benefits of deep Breathing Exercise-Times of India-Sep 13, 2017

The two most common forms of COPD are chronic bronchitis and emphysema. Chronic bronchitis is primarily characterized by a cough with mucus production that usually occurs in the winter months over two consecutive years. Chronic inflammation and narrowing of the lining of the bronchial tubes cause progressive shortness of breath, endangering the respiratory system from performing at its best. Likewise, emphysema is the destruction of the actual air sacs that are responsible for oxygen exchange. The loss of elastic fibers encompassing the air sacs causes more retained air in the chest and a distended or barrel-chest appearance. Patients present with progressive shortness of breath, a mild cough, and weight loss.[49]

On the other hand, asthma is characterized by bronchoconstriction of the airways, inflammation of the bronchial lumen, and increased mucus secretions of the airway. These three adverse events in the respiratory system cause acute shortness of breath, wheezing, tightness of the chest, and even coughing.

In addition to cigarette smokers, high rates of chronic bronchitis are found in coal miners, farmers exposed to grain, metal workers, and workers exposed to large amounts of exhaust fumes and dust.

There are environmental and genetic components to asthma exacerbation. Among the most common triggers are allergens, exercise, changes in temperature, irritants, respiratory tract infections, emotions, drugs, and occupational factors.

---

49 2005 Scientific Publishing Ltd., Rolling Meadows, Il. USA #1355

The goal of COPD patients and asthmatics are twofold: symptomatic relief and preservation of lung function. This is usually accomplished by respiratory therapy designed to promote healing of the bronchial lumen and preservation of alveolar air sacs.

———

According to the CDC eight percent of Americans suffer from seasonal allergies. Seasonal allergies manifested by sneezing, itchy eyes, coughing, a runny nose and a scratchy throat impact thirty percent of adults and forty percent of children. In severe cases rashes, hives, low blood pressure, breathing difficulty, asthma attacks and even death may occur. While there is no cure many individuals resort to immunotherapy or allergy shots to reduce the symptoms by calming down their immune systems overreaction to a foreign substance, called an allergen.

To determine the type of allergen, most individuals can have a simple prick test performed in an allergist office. Common Indoor and Outdoor allergies include:

- Cat, and dog dander

- Cockroaches

- Dust mites

- Mold spores

- Tree, grass, and weed pollen

The most common skin allergy triggers manifested as inflammation, hives, and eczema, are poison ivy, poison oak, and poison sumac.

Children have food allergies more often than adults. Most common food allergies are:

- Eggs

- Fish

- Milk

- Peanuts

- Shellfish

- Soy

- Tree nuts

- Wheat

Identifying the cause and then avoiding those allergens is the best way to manage and prevent symptoms. In addition to allergy shots, natural alternatives are equally effective.

Several natural steps can be taken to reduce allergy symptoms.

- Keep your house clean. Pollen and allergens are often present in outdoors. If you have a rug, vacuum your house regularly to remove irritants that have traveled indoors.

- Keep allergens outside. Change clothes when you get home from work or being outdoors.

- Watch the pollen count. Levels of pollen are highest early in the morning and on dry, hot, and windy days. Limit the time you spend outdoors during peak hours.

- Make your bedroom spotless. Good housekeeping habits, especially in the bedroom helps to keep allergens to a minimum.

- Knock down mold growth. Damp areas in the home can exacerbate allergies.

- Try using a mask. Wearing an air-filter mask while going outdoors can help prevent allergic reactions.

- Carry an Epi-pen. If you're at risk for life threatening anaphylaxis, (exaggerated allergic reaction to a foreign substance or allergen). Call 911 and get to the nearest emergency facility at the first sign of anaphylaxis, even if you have already administered epinephrine.[50]

50   Encyclopedia of Natural healing, Allergies and Asthma pg.178-182.

CHAPTER 8

Optimal Immunity

If at first signs of an infection you always give antibiotics, you do not give the immune system a
chance to grow stronger.

—Andrew Weil, MD

OUR BODIES' AMAZING YET COMPLEX systems of protection from
invading pathogens are our immune systems. This system's major
role is defense against viruses, fungi, parasites, and mutations. It
also assists in repairing damaged cells and destroying old cells.

Let's explore our bodies' fortified defenses as we run the race
set before us. There are two major components within our immune system: our innate and adaptive systems. Each system works
intricately with one another on behalf of our optimal health. Our
innate system, established from birth, is enhanced with nutrients
and immunoprotected factors while we are still in our mother's
womb. Immune-fighting cells called antibodies passively transfer

from the mother through the placenta to the infant in utero before we are born. This is further fortified with breast feeding during the first year of an infant's life. Studies have shown that breastfed infants have fewer infections and hospitalizations than formula-fed infants.[51] A number of health organizations including the American Academy of Pediatrics (AAP), the American Medical Association (AMA), and the World Health Organization (WHO), recommend breastfeeding as the best choice for babies. Breast feeding helps defend against infections, prevent allergies, and protect against a number of chronic conditions.[52]

Our innate (1st responders) immune system is comprised of physical barriers such as our skin and mucus membranes, as well as immune-fighting cells such as monocytes, macrophages, and leukocytes that attack foreign invaders in our body. When we are healthy, this allows our immune system to respond quickly and decisively to all immediate threats.

Our adaptive (specific responders to particular infections) immune system is stimulated by chemicals released during the innate immune response. B and T cells are activated to produce immunoglobulins to fight specific invaders called antigens. B cells (or bone marrow–derived cells) are a part of our humoral immunity and responsible for the production of antibodies. T cells are thymus-derived and responsible for cell-mediated immunity. A key feature to our adaptive immune system is memory. When

---

51 Breast feeding vs Formula Feeding; Reviewed by Elana P. Ben-Joseph, MD

52 ibid

individuals are healthy, repeat infections by the same antigen (foreign invader) are met immediately with a strong and specific response from our adaptive immune system that usually eliminates the infection. This strong and specific immune response is vital to our recovery from foreign invaders and our ability to pursue excellence in all things we desire.

Our immune system has a symbiotic relationship with the normal microbes in our gut, thereby assisting in digesting vitamins, minerals, and macronutrients used to provide fuel and energy for our body. This multilayered system of defense acts as a canopy protecting us from would be intruders. The thymus, liver, bone marrow, spleen, tonsils, lymph nodes, and blood are all involved in generating this abundant display of force, strength, and protection.

Let's navigate through this biomatrix of cellular defense and unveil its source of generating optimal health and wellness. From birth to puberty, the thymus gland, located below the sternum and between the lungs, is responsible for generating mature T cells (white blood cells) that help fight off bacteria, viruses, and fungi. While the thymus gland begins to shrink after puberty, its impact on our defense system is felt long after its role of protection and defense are done.

The core of our skeletal system consists of bone marrow that produce red blood cells (RBCs), platelets, and white blood cells (WBCs). Two main types of stem cell are contained within the skeletal system core: hematopoietic stem cells and mesenchymal stem cells. They each produce blood cells, fat cells, cartilage, and fibrous and connective tissue to form an interwoven meshwork of cells that provides the complex infrastructure of our bodies' immune system.

Specifically, hematopoietic stem cells are the gateway to healing damaged cells and organs in the human body. Whether repair, regeneration, or transplantation is required to heal damaged tissue or organs, these pluripotent cells have the genetic capacity to transform themselves into whatever is needed by the host.

This branch of regenerative medicine and stem cell research has led the way in developing new strategies to combat many chronic disease states. For years this type of research was controversial because it involved the use of embryonic tissues. However, in 2014, researchers developed a new technique to harvest stem cells from living patients. Stem cell therapy involves treating patients with their own stem cells that have been extracted, engineered to heal conditions, and then reintroduced to the body.[53]

Dr. Joshua Michael Ware, founding director of the Interdisciplinary Stem Cell Institute at the Miller School of Medicine at the University of Miami is leading many stem cell investigative treatments which he says has been nothing short of miraculous.[54] While clinical trials are ongoing, researchers found about 70 percent of the patients who received stem cell therapies demonstrated improvement without suffering negative

---

53 Encyclopedia of natural Healing, Chapter 3 Stem Cells pg.34-36; by Nick Tate: 2017

54 Ibid

side effects.[55] From type one diabetes mellitus, Parkinson's, and Alzheimer's dementia to sickle cell anemia, arthritis, spinal cord injuries, cancer, and heart and lung diseases. The possibility to dramatically alter chronic debilitating disease in our lifetime is extraordinary. Stem cell therapy is bringing new hope for natural healing that allows patients to continue to pursue their dreams, hopes, and desires.

The liver also has a prominent role in ensuring our immune systems' vitality. It provides defense-fighting Kupffer cells, which are located within the lumen of the liver sinusoids and responsible for degrading bacterial endotoxins (gut-derived bacteria and waste transported from our gastrointestinal system) and producing natural killer T cells. The role of natural killer T cells within the liver is to regulate decline in liver function and modulate liver inflammation, injury, fibrosis, and regeneration. A healthy liver with its vast functions in ensuring our bodies' peak metabolic processes, immune defense, and protection from infection is essential in our pursuit of excellence through optimal health and wellness.

Our spleen, while not a vital organ to our existence, has an equally important role in removing senescent red blood cells, storing red and white blood cells, and protecting us from certain bacterial infections. Likewise, our lymphatic system is a network of vessels containing plasma filled white blood cells designed to eliminate toxins, microbial debris, and excess fluid released from

---

55 Ibid

tissues and organs throughout our body. Each organ system involved with immunity works synergistically with one another to provide the strongest possible defense against foreign invaders.

Since our immune system is vital to our lifelong protection and pursuit of excellence, how can we do a much better job in supporting, protecting, and enhancing its efficiency and efficacy? While there is no magical supplement to enhance our immune system, our immunity evolves as we journey along life's pathway. Where we live and our companions, dietary choices, amount of exercise, age, stress management, and sleep hygiene profoundly impact the health of our immune system.

A healthy lifestyle is the best catalyst to improve the efficiency of our immune system. This includes a lack of smoking, a diet rich in fruit and green leafy vegetables, regular exercise, maintaining a healthy weight, drinking only in moderation, adequate sleep, and stress reduction. A healthy lifestyle strengthens the capability of our immune defenses' ability to protect us from all foreign invaders. In addition, foods rich in phytonutrients, antioxidants, and water-soluble vitamins A, C, E, and D enhance the performance of our immune system.

Phytonutrients are plant-derived chemical compounds that are found in colorful fruits and vegetables with antioxidant and anti-inflammatory benefits. These foods include citrus fruits, berries, mangoes, steamed broccoli (loaded with vitamins A, C, and E), garlic (rich in allicin, a potent antioxidant), ginger, turmeric (a great reducer of inflammation), green tea, steamed spinach, squash, almonds, and sunflower seeds. In contrast, processed foods high in sucrose, glucose, and fructose have shown to reduce the capacity of our immune-fighting cells to respond adequately to infection.

Ongoing studies are being performed on several food additives that are designed to enhance the shelf life, flavor, and coloring of our breads, chips, meats, dairy, corn, and sodas. Food additives and their long-term impact on our immune system are currently being investigated. Several studies have concluded that the food additive aspartame (sugar substitute) impacts the brain development in children. Monosodium glutamate (also known as MSG) increases the risk of headaches. The routine ingestion of antibiotics in cattle, swine, and poultry is being analyzed for its toxicity on the human body, increased risk of chronic disease, and immune suppression.

A prudent approach for wise consumers would be to review all labels for food additives and minimize intake of all additives as much as possible. There are also several supplements designed to enhance and boost the immune systems response to foreign invaders. Vitamins A, C, D, and E, echinacea, zinc, and elderberry are great supplements to reverse the effects of age on our immune system and enhance immunity during cold and flu season. Herbal supplements astragalus, maitake mushrooms, and olive leaf extract helps regulate the immune system, and function as an antioxidant and anti-inflammatory agent. As we pursue excellence through optimal health and wellness, our immune system is constantly evolving based on where we live, what we eat, and who our companions are. A healthy diet, and lifestyle, along with timely vaccinations throughout our life ensure the capability of a prompt immune response.

———■———

Our world, nation, and local communities are on alert. We are wrestling with an invisible, highly contagious enemy known as covid-19. Healthcare workers across our nation are in a battle to care for all those impacted by this pandemic. Whether or not universal precautions (washing of hands with soap and water, or utilizing hand sanitizer), social distancing, face mask in public places, self-quarantine or inpatient care requiring oxygen, respiratory ventilators, or renal dialysis will assist in decreasing the incidence, prevalence, and death rates of this enemy called the beast is yet to be determined. (Several intensive care unit nurses at NYU hospital have labeled covid-19 "The Beast"). Researchers are actively engaged in finding rapid testing, vaccinations and treatment modalities that will eradicate covid-19. We must each ask ourselves the question; How may we achieve optimal health? How may I strengthen my immunity? and How may I protect myself, family, and loved ones? Research studies suggest that the coronavirus is not a new virus. Quite the contrary, the coronavirus originates from a family of viruses known as SARS (Severe acute respiratory syndrome) that first appeared in China 2002. It spread worldwide via respiratory droplets but was quickly contained within several months. What has changed with the coronavirus since containment in 2002? Many studies report out of

Wuhan, China a mutation in the coronavirus which led to covid-19 and the transmission from animals to humans.[56]

Clinical manifestations of covid-19 range from being completely without symptoms (asymptomatic carrier) to a fever, cough, shortness of breath, headaches, body aches, loss of sense of taste or smell. As the virus migrates to the lower respiratory tract, oxygen saturation levels may drop well below the therapeutic range. (Normal oxygen saturation levels greater than 90%). Individuals most vulnerable appear to be the elderly, immunocompromised, or those with several chronic medical conditions. However, no one is immune. Covid-19 has impacted every race, gender, and age. And yet recent reports from the Center for Disease Control suggest that minorities with chronic medical conditions (such as asthma, poorly controlled DM, hypertension, heart disease, and severe obesity) who contract covid-19 haver a higher risk of mortality.

Our long-term goal as a nation and community must not only be the eradication of covid-19, but a shift in our perception of healthcare. Healthcare must shift from disease intervention to disease prevention and health promotion.[57] In order to accomplish this goal, we must come to appreciate the value of each human life. Each life has merit, significance and purpose. As members of society, we must become proactive in our efforts to achieve a healthier life. (Eat a healthy diet, exercise consistently, visit a

---

56 Journal of Virology,94: e00127-20; Receptor Recognition by thee Novel Coronavirus from Wuhan: an Analysis Based on Decade long Structural Studies of SARS Coronavirus, Y.Wan ,Shang J., Graham, R., Baric RS, F.Li.
57 Why Our Health Matters, A vision of medicine that can transform our future. A. Weil, MD; 2009

doctor regularly, account for any unique personal, familial, or life-style factors that can short circuit our journey such as smoking, excessive drinking, being overweight, or not getting adequate sleep.) We must continue to promote lifestyle and dietary changes that would place us each on the path to optimal health and wellness.

CHAPTER 9

Optimal Skin Health

Aging is a fact of life. Looking your age is not.

—Howard Mural, MD

ONE MANIFESTATION OF OPTIMAL HEALTH is glowing, radiant skin. Truly, the appearance of our skin speaks volumes on how well we are taking care of ourselves and our body. Let's spend a moment exploring the outward appearance of our inward grace, which we present to the world on a daily basis.

Our skin is composed of three distinct layers: the epidermis (outer layer), dermis (middle layer), and the subcutaneous tissue (innermost layer). The epidermis contains keratinocytes and melanocytes (keratin- and melanin-producing cells) that are responsible for our skin integrity and tone. The dermis, a thicker and tougher layer, contains sweat glands, hair follicles, blood vessels, and nerve fibers. Its primary role is to support the epidermis, making sure it flourishes while undergirding it with strength and elasticity by containing collagen and elastin fibers. The deeper connective tissue layer is made up of adipose tissue designed to support and cushion deeper tendons and ligaments, insulate our organs from cold, and provide the storage of fuel reserves.

When our skin is healthy and performing at its best, these three layers work in harmony with one another. The end result is a well-tuned, highly efficient system, whose functions are vast. The skin is a protective barrier and temperature regulator able to prevent internal exposure to noxious stimuli and toxins as well as protect our body from extreme heat or cold. As a large repository, our skin is able to accumulate water, fat, and metabolic products designed to prevent dehydration and produce vitamins that interact with our entire body. In addition, our skin has sensors able to detect varying degrees of pressure, expressed as dull or sharp pain, that are relayed to pain receptors within our central nervous system.

A plethora of foods, nutrients, and vitamins are essential to our skin's vibrant appearance, integrity, and optimal function. Healthy, nutritious foods that support and hydrate our skin include omega-3 fatty acids found in salmon, mackerel, and trout. Avocados, walnuts, and sunflower seeds also help to prevent ultraviolet damage from the sun. Sweet potatoes, bell peppers, tomatoes, broccoli, and soy help prevent oxidative damage and the accumulation of free radicals, which accelerate the aging process. Even dark chocolate and green tea are beneficial in enhancing the integrity of our skin!

If you prefer supplements to enhance your skin's vibrant appearance, then vitamins A, C, and E are essential to providing collagen and enhancing the flexibility of your skin. The amino acid glutamine helps to restore collagen and maintain the elasticity of our skin while also protecting our skin from ultraviolet damage and slowing the aging process. The mineral zinc and aloe from the aloe vera plant are exceptional at reducing inflammation while also promoting wound healing and repairing damaged skin. Without exception, water is essential in removing toxins and enhancing the overall metabolism of our skin and bodies. As my wife would attest, a slice of lemon in each glass of water enhances our skin's radiance and glow. Vitamin C, thank you so very much!

So how can we protect our skin against stress, ultraviolet (UV) rays from the sun, and premature aging over our lifetimes? Life can become very challenging and stressful when we attempt to pursue our dreams, goals, and aspirations or just keep life from spiraling out of control. Our bodies' response to stress under these circumstances is to produce the adrenal hormone cortisol (also known as the stress hormone), which triggers a biochemical response that activates sweat glands to secrete excessive amounts of oil to the surface of the skin, enhancing the risk of clogged pores, pimples, acne, rosacea, and other skin-related problems.

One step to prevent the ill effects of oily skin from stress is to clean the skin with an inexpensive astringent such as witch hazel several times throughout the course of a day. This simple act helps to reduce the likelihood of clogged pores, pimples, and pustules taking over our outer appearance.

Most individuals during spring or summer spend at least a few moments each day under the warmth of the sun. Whether at the golf course or swimming pool or when cycling or jogging, the effects of the sun may be gradual yet long lasting on our skin. UV rays from the sun enhance the production of melanin in our skin, tanning our complexion.

This enhanced melanin is protective and nurturing to our skin. However, excessive sun exposure may damage the elastin fibers in the skin, resulting in sagging skin that stretches, tears and prematurely ages. This weakens and destroys the skin's protective barrier and predisposes the body to increased risk of infections, abscesses, and even skin cancer.

The American Dermatology Association states that the single most important method of skin protection from UV rays is broad-spectrum, water-resistant sunscreen with a sun protective factor (SPF) greater than thirty. Equally as important is reapplying sunscreen every two hours to sustain maximum protection, even on overcast days. Other protective measures are wearing long-sleeve shirts, pants, wide-brimmed hats, and sunglasses when appropriate.[58]

UV rays are strongest between ten o'clock in the morning and two o'clock in the afternoon. So weekend warriors beware! Remember, if your shadow is shorter than you are, seek shade. Get vitamin D through a healthy diet, instead of overexposure to the sun. The risk is just too great. Lastly, avoid tanning beds;

58 Sunscreen FAQs-American Academy of Dermatology; https://www.aad.org

they too can cause premature aging, wrinkling, and skin cancer. With proper application of these simple steps, we can preserve our skin's vibrant appearance and radiance and reflect our very best in the pursuit of excellence and wellness for a lifetime.

———

According to the American Cancer Society skin cancer is the most common and preventable cancer diagnosis. While basal cell (starts in the lowest layer of skin) and squamous cell (starts in the top layer of the skin) cancers are more common, the most dangerous type of skin cancer is melanoma (starts in the color forming cells called melanocytes). Risk factors include sun exposure, sunburn, family history of skin cancer, light or pale complexion, and age. Lesions may be small, shiny, crusty, or rough. Monthly self-examination is recommended to monitor suspicious moles or changes in their size, color, or shape. It is important to remember the ABCDE rule during self-examination:

- Asymmetry (one half of the mole doesn't match the other)

- Border irregularity

- Color that is not uniform

- Diameter greater than 6 mm (about the size of a pencil eraser)

- Evolving size, shape, or color. [59]

According to the Center for Disease Control in Atlanta, Ga. The incidence of new melanoma cases continues to rise despite using sunscreen. Yale University based surgical oncologist Dr. Deepak Narayan, states sunscreen is not a magic bullet that protects us from the sun's potentially deadly rays and prevents cancer.[60] Prevention is still the key.

Seven proven ways to win the battle against melanoma.

- Limit sunburn. Avoid tanning beds and sunbathing. (especially if you have light colored eyes and fair skin.) Every five sunburns you've suffered in the past increase your risk of melanoma by 74 percent.

- Cold, cloudy days are not safe. Sun rays may be equally as intense on cloudy days and during winter months.

- Sunscreen is not armor. Look for sun protection factor of thirty. Reapply every two hours. Wear protective hats, sunglasses, and clothing.

- Boost your nutrition: Studies have shown that a diet rich in colorful fruits and vegetables helps fight cancer.

---

59 American Cancer Society-Skin Cancer Facts
60 Encyclopedia of Natural Healing: Cancer pg. 238-239; by Nick Tate 2017

- Sleep for immunity. Use the healing power of sleep to boost immunity.

- Exercise the right way: Aim for thirty minutes of exercise daily to reduce stress and boost your body's natural defenses.

- Reduce stress: Research shows that stress plays a role in lowering the body's immune system making it more susceptible to cancer.[61]

---

61 Ibid

CHAPTER 10

Optimal Women's Health

Women are the foundation of our families, the
fabric of our communities, the voice of a movement that stands up against racism, sexism, and
bullying.

—Lloyd L. Bridges, MD

MY PASSION FOR WOMEN'S HEALTH and wellness stems from
my wife and three daughters. As any parent who has raised children through years of sacrifice, unconditional love, and com-
mitment knows, the pouring out of oneself for their well-being
is paramount.

Nurturing our girls as infants; protecting their hearts, minds,
and bodies as they mature into independent thinkers and strong,
confident adults; and supporting their goals creates great joy. How
often I remembered my father's timely advice during times of
frustration or challenges with our girls. He would say, "Son, just

keep stirring the pot. Continue being kind, gentle, and patient with each of them. For it is not yet apparent who they are, or what they will become."

The American Association of University Women studied thousands of successful women and reported guidelines for raising girls for success.[62]

1. Set high educational goals. Instill in them that educational attainment is an important factor in success.

2. Help your daughters understand that they don't have to be the smartest to feel smart. Studying pays off and can lead to high achievement.

3. View your daughters as intelligent, good thinkers, and problem solvers.

4. Encourage reading, math, science, history, and social studies. Girls who thirst for learning have a better chance at success.

5. Encourage extracurricular activities such as music, art, dance, debate, and sports. Learning to manage busy schedules as a child develops organizational and planning skills as adults.

---

62 See Jane Win: The Rimm Report on How 1,000 Girls Became Successful Women; S. Rimm; April 4, 2000

6. Encourage competition to build confidence and character. Girls are often competitive. Winning builds confidence; losing builds character. Both confidence and character are needed to become successful in society.

7. Let your daughters know that popularity is not important, even if it feels that way. Nurturing independence and becoming a trend setter are even more valuable. Loneliness can be difficult during teen years. Planning fun family activities and inviting a friend helps to build family and friend bonds.

8. As parents, don't condone the use of drugs, alcohol, or smoking. The drugs of today are more potent and lethal. Make it clear that drugs and substance abuse are unacceptable. But be realistic; if they try an illegal substance, don't give up on them.

9. Remind your daughters that you are their biggest supporter and not their enemy. Guide but do not judge them. Encourage positive activities and relationships. Set firm limits but avoid over punishment.

10. Expect peaks and valleys for your daughters. Encourage perseverance, and don't overprotect because they are girls.

11. Encourage your daughters to accept the challenges that await them, to value the contributions of others and of themselves, and to explore their own creativity.

12. Enjoy the journey alongside your daughters as they grow from little girls to teenagers to successful young women.

Throughout history, women have been the catalysts to sway the pendulum toward social justice, promoting optimal health and wellness through equity, access, participation, and rights. Gender equity is fairness of treatment for men and women according to their respective needs. This includes equal treatment in terms of rights, benefits, obligations, and opportunities for advancement.

An example of gender equity has been studied extensively in the business model:

- Every 1 percent increase in gender diversity yields a 3 percent increase in revenue

- Gender-balanced companies are 15 percent more likely to outperform the industry

- Companies with more women leaders deliver a 25 percent higher return on invested capital

- "Best companies" for women have approximately 50 percent less turnover than their peers.[63]

The conclusion to gender equity and diversity is very simple. Advancing women advances and promotes businesses. It is essential through social justice that women have access to optimal health and wellness. At the core of every family is a woman's ability to care for herself and each member of the family unit through comprehensive health and preventive services.

In 2016, the Women's Preventive Service Initiative, formed by the American College of Obstetrics and Gynecology partnering with the American Academy of Family Physicians, updated essential recommendations for preventive health services in women:

1. Breastfeeding services and supplies

2. Cervical cancer screening

3. Contraception

4. Counseling for sexually transmitted infections (STIs)

5. Screening for gestational diabetes mellitus

---

63 Gender Equity: The Business Care for Women in the Boardroom; theonebrief.com

6. Screening for human immunodeficiency virus (HIV) infection

7. Screening for interpersonal and domestic violence

8. Well-woman preventive visits

9. Breast cancer screening for average-risk women

10. Screening for diabetes mellitus after pregnancy

11. Screening for urinary incontinence

As women continue to increase awareness of gender equity and diversity throughout the workplace, access to health insurance and preventive services is imperative.

Heart disease and breast cancer, both of which are preventable, are still the leading causes of a woman's premature demise. Heart disease, not cancer, is the number one cause of death among women as they age. In fact, one of five women will die of heart disease, regardless of race.[64] While more men have heart attacks at age sixty-five, the number of women who have a heart attack at age seventy-two has almost doubled. Many research studies suggest that menopause and the loss of the protective hormone estrogen plays a critical role in this finding. In fact, low HDL

---

64 Women and Heart Disease; https://www.cdc.gov

and high triglycerides increase the risk of death from heart disease in women over age sixty-five. In addition, poorly controlled diabetes mellitus, and metabolic syndrome (large waist, elevated blood pressure, glucose intolerance, low HDL, and high triglycerides) produce a much greater cardiovascular risk for women than men.[65] However, the burden of stress, poor dietary habits, sedentary lifestyle, alcohol abuse, and cigarette smoking are also identifying triggers that cannot be ignored.

Research studies report that after a first heart attack, 47 percent of women will die within five years. With men, this statistic is only 36 percent. This suggest that women are not being treated as aggressively as men once hospitalized for heart attacks; women seek medical attention much later than men (fifty-four hours after symptom development for women versus sixteen hours for men), and women's symptoms are less classic than men. Most men present with the classic midsternal chest heaviness, with pain radiating up the neck and down the left shoulder and arm. However, many women, in addition to chest discomfort, may present with less ominous symptoms of shortness of breath, nausea, dizziness, and fatigue.[66] Preventive care through dietary modifications, regular exercise, weight management, smoking cessation, effective stress management, and proper sleep hygiene are key factors in reducing a woman's risk for heart disease and living a long healthy life.

---

65   About Heart Disease in Women; redforwomen.org
66   ibid

Breast disease: Breast cancer is the second most common cancer diagnosed in women and the second leading cause of cancer death after lung cancer.

According to the National Cancer Institute, there are several well-established risk factors for developing breast cancer:

1. Age greater than fifty

2. Prior history or family history of breast cancer

3. The start of an early menstrual cycle, before age twelve

4. Late menopause, after age fifty

5. No children (nulliparity)

6. Age greater than thirty at first birth

7. Obesity (BMI greater than thirty)

8. High socioeconomic status

9. Abnormal cells on breast biopsy

10. Exposure to ionizing radiation

There are many signs of breast disease. Detection of a breast mass is the most common presenting symptom. However, 90 percent of these lesions are noncancerous fibroadenomas. Redness, swelling, nipple discharge, and retraction of the nipple are potential signs of breast cancer. A unilateral mass that is solid, hard, and fixed to the surrounding breast tissue is very suspicious for malignancy.

The United States Preventive Services Task Force recommends screening mammography every two years for women ages fifty to seventy-four.[67]

Electing to screen prior to age fifty should be an individual choice based on well-established risk factors. Women with a parent, sibling, or child with breast cancer would benefit from earlier screening in their forties. Genetic testing has become a tool to identify women who have a high risk for breast cancer through BRCA gene analysis. There is insufficient evidence to screen women age seventy-five or older because harms may outweigh the benefits.

Patient education, accessibility to diagnostic imaging, and preventive health services are vital components in the early detection of breast cancer at a stage when it is both curable and lifesaving.

---

67   Breast Cancer: Screenin Recommendation; www.uspreventiveservice-taskforce January 20216

Menopause: Most women experience a slow decline in estrogen production by the ovaries between the age of forty and fifty-five. Surgically induced menopause may occur before age forty if both ovaries and the uterus are removed as a result of severe pelvic pain and its complications.[68]

There are three phases of menopause:

1. Perimenopause occurs over several years when the estrogen and progesterone levels begin to decline and the menstrual cycle becomes more erratic (with changes in the length and flow of the cycle). Perimenopause also leads to missed cycles, hot flashes, and emotional and cognitive changes.

2. Menopause is signaled when estrogen production is too low to initiate a menstrual cycle and periods stop completely.

3. Postmenopause, also known as true menopause, occurs when a menstrual cycle has not occurred for twelve months.

The role of estrogen: The most potent form of estrogen is estradiol, which is responsible for female characteristics and sexual reproductive development. Estradiol plays a vital role in the female genital tract's ability to sustain a favorable environment for the survival of sperm during the menstrual cycle. Estradiol

---

68 Understanding Menopause; 2005 Scientific Publishing Ltd, Rolling Meadows, Il. USA #5500

also stimulates the growth of breast tissue, improves blood flow by preventing high blood pressure, and supports the integrity of the skeletal system by assisting in retaining calcium in bone. Estrogen levels peak during puberty, initiating a women's reproductive years, then slowly begin to decline after age forty, signaling the perimenopausal phase.[69]

Body changes during menopause: One of the most prevalent changes during menopause is the gradual thinning and drying of the genitourinary tract, including the vagina, vulva, and urethra. In addition, there is loss of breast tissue firmness, size, and shape. There is also weakening of the pelvic ligaments that may result in urinary incontinence. Hair may become thinner, while the skin may become drier as it loses some of its elasticity. There may also be loss of bone density, resulting in an increased risk of osteoporosis.[70]

———

Emotional and cognitive impact during menopause: Hormonal changes during menopause may result in mood and cognitive challenges that may be brief, over several weeks, or of longer duration, several years. These changes include heightened anxiety or panic attacks, mood swings, short-term memory lapses, depression, difficulty focusing, or decreased libido (sex drive).[71]

---

69   ibid
70   ibid
71   ibid

Therapeutic options for menopausal symptoms: Hormonal replacement therapy (HRT) and bioidentical hormone therapy are treatment options to reduce the intensity and incidence of hot flashes and the risk for osteoporosis and postmenopausal heart disease.

In addition, natural supplements such as isoflavones, soy, black cohosh, licorice, and red clover have shown to reduce menopausal symptoms with varying results. Healthy eating habits, regular exercise, stress management, and proper sleep hygiene are important factors as women age gracefully and sustain optimal health and wellness.

As more women seek career-family balance and challenge old stereotypes while leading in the areas of business, banking, politics, medicine, law, education, religion, and the arts, it is imperative that optimal health and wellness be the impetus that complements a women's passions and enhances her pursuits of excellence in all the things she desires.

CHAPTER 11

Optimal Men's Health

Remember your creator in the days of your youth, for the days of trouble come, and the years approach, when you will say, "I find no pleasure in them."

—Ecclesiastes 12:1(NIV)

OPTIMAL HEALTH DURING OUR YOUTH brings a freedom to explore, conquer, and achieve all that we imagine and desire. As males our youth fuels our passions and dreams to unveil the mysteries of our hearts' proclivities. As boys mature into adolescence and young adulthood, it is the predominance of the male hormone testosterone, coupled with lower estradiol levels, that is responsible for continued growth and development, including enlargement of the penis and testicles, increased body and facial hair, and enhanced muscle mass and bone strength.[72]

Testosterone production is triggered by hormones from the hypothalamus, a small region in the brain that coordinates the neuroendocrine pathways to the pituitary gland. The pituitary gland, a tiny structure located within the base of the brain, stimulates reproductive hormones within the anterior pituitary. This pathway stimulates the testes to produce testosterone, which promotes sperm production, sexual function, and secondary sexual characteristics.[73]

Normal or healthy levels of testosterone circulating in the bloodstream are between 300 and 1,100 nanograms per deciliter (ng/dL) for adult males and between 15 and 70 ng/dL for adult females.[74] Testosterone levels peak in men between eighteen and twenty years of age. A slow, precipitous decline of testosterone occurs after the age of thirty. There are instances when testosterone levels peak before the age of eighteen (precocious puberty) or after the age of twenty (delayed puberty).

What happens when men become emotionally detached, uncommitted, and dispassionate in most areas of their lives? Low testosterone may have occurred. It may be so subtle that it's not even acknowledged. Most men are too embarrassed to even consider

72 Bhasin S, Cunningham GR, Hayes FJ,et al. Testosterone therapy in adult men with androgen deficiency syndromes: an Endocrine Society clinical practice guideline. J Clin Endocrinol Metab. 2010;95:2536-2559
73 ibid
74 Mulligan T, Frick MF, Zuraw QC, Stemhagen A. McWhirter C. Prevalence of hypogonadism in males at least 45 years: the HIM study. Int J Clin Pract. 2006; 60:762-769.

themselves as having low testosterone (T). Whenever testosterone levels drop below normal, a signaling problem may have occurred between the brain and testes or even the testes themselves.

Clinical clues to low T include the following:

1. Mental fatigue (brain fog)

2. Heightened agitation (decreased mood)

3. Decrease in muscle mass/strength

4. Decrease in bone strength

5. Reduced sexual drive or libido

6. Sexual dysfunction[75]

There are several medical conditions that increase the likelihood of developing low T:

1. Obesity (body mass index greater than thirty)

2. Diabetes mellitus (hemoglobin A1c greater than 6.5)

3. High cholesterol

---

75 ibid

4. Hypertension (Blood pressure higher than 140/90)

5. Asthma or COPD[76]

There are several misconceptions about erectile dysfunction and low T. While they may overlap, everyone that experiences erectile dysfunction (an inability to obtain or sustain an erection during coitus) does not necessarily have low T. Remember, cardiovascular disease may also cause erectile dysfunction. While it is common for testosterone levels to diminish with age, levels falling below the normal range are not a natural part of the aging process. Therefore, healthy men above the age of sixty-five should enjoy intimacy naturally with their significant others.

In addition to dietary modifications and regular exercise, vitamin D, zinc, fenugreek, and ashwagandha are supplements shown to naturally enhance testosterone levels. While marketing has done a masterful job in promoting testosterone replacement therapy, there are several precautions that must be weighed before taking the testosterone replacement therapy (TRT) leap.

Several potential adverse effects may occur as a result of testosterone replacement therapy:

1. Enhanced red blood cell production by the bone marrow may cause blood clots, increasing the risk of heart attacks or strokes.

---

76 ibid

2. Chronic TRT may increase the risk of liver toxicity.

3. Chronic TRT may reduce the body's ability to produce its own testosterone resulting in infertility. Men desiring to start a family naturally would not want to pursue this option.

4. Chronic TRT may increase the risk of breast tenderness and swelling, a condition known as gynecomastia, and even testicular atrophy or shrinkage.[77]

While TRT may assist in producing a stronger physique and enhanced libido, not all men are candidates for TRT. Do you, or a first degree relative, have a history of breast or prostate cancer? Are you at risk for heart or liver disease? If so, then TRT may not be for you. Ongoing research is underway to determine the risk stratification of TRT based on age, race, and other health-related conditions.

———■———

Prostate health: This exocrine gland that is often forgotten during our youthful vigor and conquest plays a vital role in the transportation of sperm during ejaculation. This small gland, about the size of an apricot, is located immediately below the urinary

---

77 Adverse effects of testosterone replacement therapy: an update on. The evidence and controversy https://www.ncbi.nlm.nih.gov >pmc

bladder, allowing the urethra to traverse directly through the prostate and penis. A healthy prostate gland allows most men to experience the pleasures of an intimate relationship. The release of seminal fluid containing citric acid and zinc enhances sperm mobility within the ejaculate.

There are several healthy foods designed to promote prostate health and reduce the risk of developing prostate cancer:

1. Tomatoes: Tomatoes contain the powerful antioxidant lycopene that destroys free radicals and prevents the growth of many cancer-causing cells.

2. Lentils: Lentils (or beans) are a type of insoluble fiber thought to cleanse the body of toxins and reduce the risk of prostate cancer.

3. Broccoli: Cruciferous vegetables, such as broccoli, enhance gene expression in prostate tissue to lower the risk of prostate cancer.

4. Green tea: Green tea contains properties that reduce inflammation of the prostate and improve urinary flow.

5. Pomegranate juice: Some studies show a decrease in the rate of the rise of the prostate-specific antigen (PSA) with consistent oral consumption, which reduces the risk of prostate enlargement.

6. Salmon: Omega-3 fatty acids found in salmon are thought to enhance prostate health and reduce the proliferation of tumor-producing cells in the prostate.[78]

Studies have shown that, 70 percent of men above fifty-five years of age will develop urinary urgency and frequency, decreased urinary stream, and/or excessive dribbling after urination. These are all symptoms associated with an enlarged prostate gland. Younger men that are generally healthy with these urinary symptoms may have increased risk of prostatitis (an infection of the prostate gland).

There has been quite a debate in the medical literature over whether screening for prostate cancer should occur because of the percentage of false positive results. The United States Preventive Service Task Force (USPSTF) recommendations for prostate cancer screening are as follows: "For men aged 55 to 69 years, the decision to undergo periodic prostate-specific antigen (PSA)–based screening for prostate cancer should be an individual one."[79]

Before deciding whether to be screened, men should have an opportunity to discuss the potential benefits and harms of screening with their clinician and to incorporate their values and preferences in the decision. Screening offers a small potential benefit of reducing the chance of death from prostate cancer in some men. Clinicians should not screen men who do not express a preference for screening. The USPSTF recommends against

---

78 Six foods to boost Prostate Health – Healthline Mar29,2017
79 Screening for Prostate Cancer: USPSTF; May 8,2018

PSA-based screening for prostate cancer in men seventy years and older.[80]

According to researchers from the Fred Hutchinson Cancer Research center in Seattle, Washington, black men have a 60 percent greater risk of developing and dying from prostate cancer than their white counterparts. In addition, prostate cancer advances much faster in black men than white men. Screening recommendations for the general population are not optimal for black men. After discussing with your healthcare provider, black men should consider screening in their forties, and more frequently.

———■———

Protecting our children: Too often in a quest for significance, fame, and prosperity men lose sight of their family and beloved children along the journey. Without love, guidance, direction, or leadership, children are often left to go astray. If men are blessed to have children, it is imperative that men remain engaged in their lives, protecting them from every heinous, destructive force under the sun—from bullying, social media, and its exploits to verbal, physical, or sexual abuse. Men must stand in the gap for their children.

Caregivers must provide a loving home and nourishment for children physical and emotional well-being. We must protect their

80 ibid

dreams and encourage their creativity. We must support and develop their gifts and talents. We must listen to their fears and reassure them of a better tomorrow. We must restrain the forces of evil and corruption that seek to derail our children while pouring unconditional love into their hearts daily. As caregivers, we must stand in the gap between yesterday's mistakes and tomorrow's promises. We must trust the process and allow time to transform our children's dreams into reality.

———

How do we allow our destiny cloaked in our mind's imagination, refined by the fires of life, to become our absolute truth? It must be understood that obstacles, setbacks, and even misfortunes are interwoven in the refining process. At times, self-doubt and even uncertainty may enter our thoughts as we pursue excellence in all aspects of our lives. However, if we remain hopeful and resilient, despite being excluded or dismissed, then our dreams will become reality. Remember, our destiny is interwoven with the challenges that we face and the resistance that we overcome. This refining process shapes our journey and molds our path until we evolve into our best selves in our pursuit of excellence in all things we desire.

CHAPTER 12

Optimizing Spiritual Wellness

If I speak in the tongues of men and of angels
but have not love, I am only a resounding gong
or clanging symbol. If I have the gift of prophecy
and can fathom all mysteries and all knowledge,
and if I have a faith that can move mountains, but
have not love, I am nothing. If I give all I possess
to the poor and surrender my body to the flames,
but have not love, I gain nothing.

—1 Corinthians 13:1–3 (NIV)

MANY SCIENTIST BELIEVE WE, AS humans, are an interwoven col-
lection of carbon molecules defined by the molecular structure of
our DNA and interacting with our universe and the kinetic energy
surrounding our environment. And yet we are so much more!
Yes, fully molecular, spiritual beings encased in earthly human
vessels for a season. We are designed to fulfill our chosen destiny,

longing for love, companionship, acceptance, and compassion for our fellow man.

If we are indeed spirit, what then defines our spirituality? Is spirituality a composite reflection of our memories and the depth of our joys, passions, and fears? Or is spirituality our faith, beliefs, values, principles, and morals manifested in the recesses of our mind and expressed through our daily experiences? Can our spirituality be linked to our invisible thoughts that shape our existence and current reality? Is our spirituality connected with our behavior and the convergence of our environment, intellect, occupation, and social and financial well-being?

The United States Department of Health and Human Services Substance Abuse and Mental Health Services Administration has defined dimensions of wellness that encompass a comprehensive view of optimal health and spirituality.

Whether we are in an urban or rural setting, our environment and how we respond to environmental triggers, such as crime, air pollution, garbage buildup, or natural disasters, determines the trajectory of our health and life span. We truly become one with our environment and thrive when our parks, rivers, and even the air we breathe are free of pollution, debris, and toxic waste. We are at our best when we can embrace our surroundings with love and respect for our environment.

The ability to respond to the unexpected in life and sustain long-term financial security for ourselves and our families is essential in reducing stress and managing effectively all of life's challenges. Building a sustainable legacy to pass on to our children and grandchildren is an essential component of wealth management and preserving optimal health in our families for generations. Developing philanthropic efforts to give back to, support, and sustain our communities is vital to our neighborhoods survival.

Plan ahead by protecting your family, your assets, and your home in the event you are incapacitated or laid off or suffer an untimely death. Adequate life, medical, home, and auto insurance is paramount. Our families deserve our best preparation.

Cultivating our minds, exploring our dreams, navigating our imaginations and depth of passion for life is our quest for intellectual development. Embracing contrasting views stimulates thoughtful ideas and discussion in our ever-changing complex world. As we evolve and mature in wisdom and understanding, we are able to engage the complexities of our current time and impact our families, communities, and world for generations to come.

We are social beings longing to communicate and interact with others by giving of our time, talents, and resources. Giving is actually what we do best. Through local charitable groups, churches, sororities, fraternities, and philanthropic efforts, we are able to positively impact our communities. One of our greatest gifts is our ability to connect with our fellow man and give unselfishly to those less fortunate than ourselves. Saint Francis of Assisi said, "For it is in giving that we truly receive." Giving is the master key to success in life.

Our occupation allows us to fulfill our dreams, hopes, and aspirations and provide for our families. It also allows us to network and interact with our peers based on core values and skill sets.

Collaborating with our colleagues and setting work-related goals enhances satisfaction and value to our job. Positioning ourselves to reach others while making a positive impact in our communities is rewarding and fulfilling.

Our intellectual capacity is determined by genetic and environmental factors. Our desire to serve others is determined through selfless acts of kindness. Using our intellect to cure diseases and solve the crisis of anger, indifference, boasting, and man's inhumanity to one another, rather than exploiting those less gifted than ourselves, should be our aim.

As we strive for spiritual enlightenment in our pursuit of excellence, it is our journey rather than our appointed destination that defines the richness of our experience. Our challenge is to understand that we are not alone in our pursuit of excellence through optimal health and wellness.

If we can endure wrong with patience and kindness, consistently resisting corruption with conviction; if we can enjoy all that is pleasant with enthusiasm and continue giving unselfishly of ourselves with humility; if we can nurture others with compassion and rejoice in their accomplishment; if we can pursue excellence, shunning mediocrity and apathy, refusing to cut corners in our quest for optimal health and wellness—then we can become fearless in our pursuits, courageous in our efforts, and bold enough to speak our desires into existence with perseverance and tenacity. Our minds, bodies, and spirits are designed, equipped, and prepared to uniquely achieve our dreams, hopes, and aspirations.

What may seem impossible to others is attained with a joy and passion that cannot be explained by spectators or casual observers.

How can our best be attained in a world of chaos, cynicism, and pessimism? It can be attained by plunging ourselves into our creative genius and being resolute and determined about our pursuits, desires, and destiny, and thoroughly committed to a life of hope, faith, and love. If we can embrace these virtues in our pursuits of excellence, then we will never, ever settle for anything less than our best.

I believe that Dr. Benjamin Elijah Mays, a president emeritus of Morehouse College, eloquently described this when he put pen to parchment and wrote:

> I have only just a minute,
> Only sixty seconds in it.
> Forced upon me, can't refuse it.
> Didn't seek it, didn't choose it.
> But it's up to me to use it.
> I must suffer if I lose it.
> Give account if I abuse it.
> Just a tiny little minute,
> But eternity is in it.[81]

---

81 Benjamin E. Mayes I've only just a minute, https://www.fultonleadershipacademy.com

One final thought as we pursue excellence through optimal health and wellness: let us live, laugh, and love each day to its fullest!

Much joy,

Your Family Doc!

Acknowledgments

WITH SPECIAL THANKS AND GRATITUDE:

To my beloved wife, Tamara (Lil Momma) Bridges: Your unconditional love and sacrifice has sustained me throughout my medical career and helped me to complete this book.

To my three girls, Nia, Carin, and Amaya: With joy, you all make everything worthwhile.

To Novant Health and Our Health, who provided the canvas for me to serve my Heavenly Father through the practice of medicine.

To the Park and Elevation Church, Bishop Claude R. Alexander, and Pastor Steve Furtick for providing a fresh anointing for my family throughout the years.

To (The Ly-On Nine) of Omega Psi Phi fraternity Inc., Psi chapter, for forging a bond of brotherhood and support for one another.

To the 305, Raider Nation, Morehouse tigers, and the U (Univ of Miami), for all my teachers, classmates, and friends for supporting me along my journey.